THE DON'T SWEAT GUIDE
TO GOLF

Other books by the editors of Don't Sweat Press

The Don't Sweat Affirmations
The Don't Sweat Guide for Couples
The Don't Sweat Guide for Graduates
The Don't Sweat Guide for Grandparents
The Don't Sweat Guide for Parents
The Don't Sweat Guide for Moms
The Don't Sweat Guide for Weddings

THE DON'T SWEAT GUIDE TO GOLF

Playing Stress-Free So You're at the Top of Your Game

By the Editors of Don't Sweat Press
Foreword by Richard Carlson, Ph.D.,
author of the bestselling *Don't Sweat the Small Stuff*

HYPERION

New York

Hyperion books are available for special promotions and premiums.
For details contact Hyperion Special Markets, 77 West 66th Street,
11th floor, New York, New York, 10023, or call 212-456-0100.

ISBN 0-7868-8783-4

FIRST EDITION

10 9 8 7 6 5 4 3 2 1

Contents

Foreword

More than a game, golf is a celebration of life. It's supposed to be fun! Sometimes, however, in our quest to improve our game, some of us take it a tiny bit too seriously and that sense of fun begins to disappear. In other words, there's a fine line between improvement that is "worth it," and attempts to improve that result in the reduction or even elimination of the "fun factor." Ideally, we can strike the perfect balance. I believe this book can help make that happen.

Golf is a beautiful game that speaks to the essence of life. When you're playing well, you're absolutely "present," fully absorbed in the moment—just like when you're living life to its fullest. On the one hand, you're relaxed. On the other, you're super focused and non-distracted. You are patient and willing to wait.

Golfers have told me that when they are playing their best, they are in the flow of the game. Even difficult shots feel good—drives and putts are struck with precision. When appropriate, they are strong and deliberate. Other times, it's all about a soft touch, really knowing the course.

The editors of Don't Sweat Press have written what I believe to be an excellent and very unique guide to golf. The selections were created to add inspiration and insight to one of the great games in the world! In addition, because many golfers, at every level of play, experience at least some stress while playing, the strategies in this book can help us approach the game with heightened perspective, and even a bit of humor. What's more, the wisdom of this book can enhance many aspects of your life, beyond the golf course.

I congratulate you for choosing such a great game as one of your hobbies and passions. My wish is that you will be able to enjoy the game of golf for the rest of your life. I hope this book reinforces the joy you receive from the game and gives you a tiny edge in all aspects of your life.

Treasure the gift of golf,
Richard Carlson
Benicia, California
January 2002

THE DON'T SWEAT GUIDE
TO GOLF

1.

Remember That
It's Just a Game

There is no other game, sport, recreational pastime, or hobby that compares to golf. No two courses are alike, the game is played amidst a natural setting, and golf requires a combination of great mental and physical ability to conquer. It's no secret that a lot of golfers take the game very seriously. When you begin to take it too seriously, however, it helps to remember the reasons that you began playing in the first place.

There are so many reasons to play golf. Perhaps you want more exercise or a way to relax. You might enjoy the friendly competition and camaraderie provided by a good game of golf with friends. Whatever your reasons for taking up the game, it's certain that the word "fun" is in there somewhere. As you learn and grow with the game of golf, it's crucial that you don't lose sight of that tiny three-letter word.

Everyone plays golf to have fun. Yet golfers can become so wrapped up in how they play, what their scores are, how much better (or worse) they are than their partners, or how much they're improving that the concept of fun disappears. The need for perfection takes any and all enjoyment out of the game. Competition with others—and yourself—can take precedence over the feeling of freedom that you can get from walking a beautifully designed course on a warm spring morning.

If you find yourself getting tense, angry, or frustrated on the golf course, you've taken a wrong turn somewhere. Golf was never meant to ruin you emotionally. Rather it should calm and soothe the soul, and give you a respite from the craziness of the outside world. It's a game. Recreation. In the big picture of life, it should be kept in that perspective.

The game of golf has always been compared to the game of life. Golfer Gardner Dickinson once said, "They say that life is a lot like golf—don't believe them. Golf is a lot more complicated." Take that statement in the same spirit that it was most assuredly spoken: with tongue planted firmly in cheek. Enjoying the game of golf is easy, as long as you never lose sight of the fact that it really, truly is just a game.

2.

Resist the Urge to
Criticize Other Players

You can probably find more free advice and criticism on a golf course than almost any other place. Advice is usually offered in good faith toward the idea of helping someone improve. But criticism has a bite to it, a sharp edge that others rarely appreciate.

Being a critic on the golf course has the potential to ruin more than a few friendships. If you play frequently, you have probably noticed that all the criticism in the world does nothing to make someone a better player, move the game along any faster, or add to anyone's fun.

If you find yourself criticizing other players, understand that it can become a familiar habit. But a habit can be broken. The best way to do that is to remember how you feel whenever someone criticizes you. You may also find that you don't feel good yourself after you've pronounced judgment on others. Learn to catch yourself in the act of being critical, and see if you can turn it off. You may find that you'll have more friends on the course, and you'll feel better about yourself.

3.

The Score
Isn't Everything

Do you ever think that golfers might be a little too obsessed with keeping score? True, you can't maintain a handicap without keeping score, nor can you compare recent rounds with past efforts. In fact, the USGA requires that all rounds be recorded to create and maintain a handicap. But players often take all the fun out of the game by making the score the only thing that's important.

Your score is a measure of how well or poorly you're playing, and it's natural to want to improve it—but constantly obsessing about it certainly takes away from your fun. The "card and pencil" mentality places too much importance on the size of the numbers and not enough on skill and pleasure. Thus, beginning your round on a less-than-stellar note can often lead to a sense of frustration and malaise by the third or fourth hole! If your enjoyment of the game comes only from what's on the scorecard, you're truly missing the real pleasures: camaraderie, the beauty and challenge of a well-designed course, fresh air, exercise, and an opportunity to improve, no matter how good you already are.

The great Bobby Jones has said, "The real way to enjoy playing golf is to take pleasure not in the score, but in the execution of the strokes." In other words, each new stroke offers an opportunity to excel not by the numbers, but by your skill and finesse. Ignoring the score, you can be motivated to strive consistently throughout the game without feeling defeated from the start. See if you and your partners can ease up on the scorekeeping obsession. It can make the game more enjoyable for everyone.

4.

Remind Yourself That
Everyone Was Once a Beginner

If you're just starting out in the game of golf, you might feel a little anxious to get to the point where you will no longer call yourself a beginner. Just remember that everyone had to start somewhere. When your stroke is giving you problems or you can't manage to make contact with the ball, remind yourself that everyone has traveled along the learning curve—even the pros who make it look so easy.

You can't expect to play like Greg Norman in your first few months. It takes time and practice to tune in to the finer aspects of the game. Understand that you'll make a lot of mistakes, and that's okay, because everyone who picks up a club and walks a course makes mistakes. How you react to those mistakes is what counts. You can learn to become an angry, reactive player, or you can learn to view each mistake as an opportunity to improve.

The trick to becoming a calm, relaxed player is to have patience from the start. Don't get too worked up or concerned about how you're doing, where you're hitting, or how far. Get comfortable with the basics of stance, grip, and swing while you learn and practice the rules of etiquette. Watch the pros, but watch other players at your club, too. Spend time on the driving range—it's the perfect place to learn the strokes of this awkward game before trying your luck on a course.

Golf is a physical and mental game that can bring you a lifetime of pleasure. Learning it is a process. As you move through the steps, you might experience occasional setbacks. Try to stay calm. Use your greatest learning opportunities to grow and gain perspective on your game. You will come to love the game more each time that you play. If you feel like you're the only beginner in the bunch, try picturing your favorite pros as beginners. It may help you to see that every golfer once traveled the path that you're on.

5.

Refuse to
Let Noise Distract You

Others' talking and whispering while you're planning your drive; throat-clearing, coughing, or sniffling while you putt; Velcro ripping, humming, whistling, and squeaking shoes—these are all distractions on the golf course that can drive you crazy if you let them! Learning to tune out noise and keep your annoyance in check is essential to this game of great concentration. Golf is a game of precision, timing, and accuracy with little room for mistakes. If others around you are making noise or otherwise distracting you from your play with disastrous results, how can it possibly not irritate you? But beware the knee-jerk reaction, because you may later regret it.

When we overreact, it's often because we are confronted with things that are out of our control. Face it: You can't control players who aren't mindful of etiquette, nor can you control spectators who don't understand enough about etiquette to avoid making distracting mistakes. Getting angry only compounds the problem. You lose your focus, poorly execute a shot, and blow the rest of your day.

The idea isn't to deny that something bugs you when it really does, but rather to retrain yourself to be less reactive, to respond differently. If you know that you have a distracting player in your group, you might tell yourself in advance, "I won't be bothered or overreact to her behavior." You may not be convinced that this is enough to keep you from being bothered, but practice it with the understanding that your reactions are largely habitual. Habits can be broken.

Give this strategy a try, and have patience. You may be surprised to find out just how effective it can be. You'll enjoy your game much more when you stop allowing distractions to bother you.

6.

Learn to
Laugh at Yourself

Golf is not only humbling, it is also a deeply frustrating game.
Anyone who has picked up a club and played a few holes
knows that when the going gets tough, you can get anxious. The
more tense you become, the harder it is to concentrate on your shot
and do your best. Some days you can overcome the frustrations
more easily than others. You can have a few good shots for every
bad one, rack up a decent score, and feel fine. But other days, you
just can't shake the bad vibes. On those days, there may be little
you can do but laugh at yourself.

Sometimes, laughing at yourself is the best—if not the only—
way to get through a bad round. On those days when you simply
can't hit anything but a top, or constantly blow two-foot putts,
being able to look back on the round and laugh will keep you from
becoming so frustrated that you give up the game. It does happen—
some golfers can't learn to control their frustrations and let their

anger get the best of them. They quit the game, feeling that they'll never become better players.

The truth is that learning to laugh at yourself can help you become a better player. When you can find humor in your faults and not take your mistakes too seriously, it's easier to relax and work out your problems. You can channel your anger toward solving those problems, turning it into determination that will help you approach your practice sessions with a level head and a steady nerve. Keeping a sense of humor helps you remember that it is a game, after all, and you're supposed to have fun with it.

It can't hurt to spread this philosophy around a little. Anything you can do to help reduce the number of hotheads on the course and the practice range is good. The next time one of your partners seems to be taking himself and his game a bit too seriously, see if you can help him laugh. Just do so carefully—remember that there are plenty of golfers out there who have a hard time turning their yips, slices, and shanks into things that they can laugh at.

7.

Skip the
Hole-by-Hole Accounts

Golfers belong to a large fraternity of sorts. They speak their own language, and they all understand the problems of their brothers and sisters who play the game. They can relate to the thrills experienced by fellow golfers, and they may willingly listen to stories about good days on the links. Despite being competitors, they can even sympathize when their compatriots are struggling. However, one sure way to aggravate and bore most golfers is to assume that they want to hear hole-by-hole accounts of your golf rounds.

Golfers go through a stage in which they're so infatuated by the game that they think there's nothing finer in life than sharing the most minute details about their rounds. Sure, your golfing friends will want to listen to a fun story about your day, your eighteen-hole score, and a few comments about the course. But it's crucial to understand that they don't want to go through all eighteen holes, and probably no one does.

A hole-by-hole recount is one of those things that can ruin friendships, business relationships, and golf foursomes—maybe more so than slow play or a triple bogey that's reported on the scorecard as a par. So leave out the forty-five-minute account of the first time you broke 80. It's okay to talk about a great hole or two, or even a terrible one. But if the people around you say, "Are we going to go all eighteen?" then you know they've picked up on clues that you're about to go too far.

Getting bitten by the golf bug or the euphoria of finally playing well can be overwhelming to others. Catching yourself before you become a "golf cliché" will prevent irritation in others and make sure that everyone still enjoys playing a round with you.

8.

Play the Wind

There are some things in life—and golf—that you can't control, and Mother Nature is one of them. Windy days can be a tremendous source of frustration on the golf course, making the ball drop out of the sky like a lead brick. Other times, the wind can be a great ally, carrying the ball farther and more precisely than you might have imagined you could hit it. The wind, like life, is always changing. Learning to adapt to the changes can help you play the wind more strategically and with less frustration.

You might try thinking of the wind as an essential element of the game. In fact, many early pioneers of golf thought that it was the most essential element, noting that without the wind, a particular course was always the same. With varying wind, you play not one course, but many. As course design has changed, so has the modern view of wind as part of the game. Once essential, today it's more often seen as an unfair, unpredictable thorn in the side of the player, interfering with an otherwise great game.

If you are mentally flexible, you can go with the flow and learn to love the wind. Some days it's with you, and other days it's undoubtedly against you. Either way, you can play more calmly and with more enjoyment if you work with the wind rather than against it. Remember that golf is as much a contest against nature and the elements as it is against the field, the architect, and the superintendent. The wind—no matter what you think of it or how unlucky its effects—is nature's contribution to that contest.

You can take consolation from the fact that you're not alone on a windy day—everyone else is feeling the wind's effects, too. It's likely that nobody will get quite the distance they're used to. After all, golf is a game of odds, and when it's windy, they're stacked against everyone.

9.

As You Warm Up, Think
Tempo, Not Results

How you warm up on the practice range can set the tone for your entire round. You can defeat yourself from the start if you go into your warm-up with results in mind, rather than focusing on the things that can make your game better and more enjoyable.

Formulating expectations as a result of your warm-up can get you into trouble. You may or may not play as well or as poorly as you have warmed up. The point is to loosen up, find a rhythm, and whet your appetite for the round ahead. You cannot compare the work that you do on a golf course rife with hazards to the driving range, a big open field where alignment, distance, and concentration don't even come into play.

The best thing that you can do when warming up is to set a pace for yourself. Focusing on tempo is the trick to avoiding any kind of expectations about your upcoming game—good or bad. The emotional swings that affect your play are usually based on your expectations. If you avoid setting yourself up, then you'll feel a lot better about yourself and your game.

10.

You Have to
Play the Ball Where It Lies

This is a fundamental rule of golf, yet many players seem to have a problem with it. Usually, that problem occurs whenever they land in a divot or a hazard, or when they simply don't like the way that the ball sits on top of the fairway.

While the breaks may sometimes be unfair, accept that this is part of the game. Architects have even designed courses with this in mind. Thus the really interesting holes are quite often the ones where unlikely things happen. They may seem awful at the time that they occur, but if you stop and think about it, they probably become the stories that you remember best and laugh about most later on. These are also the holes that turn out to be the most challenging and fun.

You do have an option: If the lie is that bad, you can always take a penalty stroke under the unplayable lie rule. But why not rise to the challenge of bringing that ball out of the tough spot in the best way you can? That's truly why you love the game of golf, after all.

If golf is indeed a great metaphor of life, then "play the ball where it lies" is truly a way of accepting what comes your way. There's hardly a better example than when golfer Bobby Jones was diagnosed with a rare and degenerative central nervous disease that disabled him. In great pain, and unable to walk or play golf, Jones was asked in an interview if he was resentful. He answered: "We play the ball where it lies."

11.

Play the Hole
That You're On

There is no bigger waste of time, energy, and concentration than worrying about what might happen on the next hole. Getting nervous with "what if?" thoughts and overblown images of upcoming holes can make your worst playing nightmares come true right where you're standing. Additionally, the stress and anxiety can be passed on to your playing partners, ruining the game for everyone.

Learning to play the hole that you're on and blocking out what lies ahead can be summed up in a simple concept: Live (and play) in the moment. This "one-hole-at-a-time" thinking can push aside reactive concerns and focus your concentration where it should be—on the play at hand. Your play will be calm and peaceful, and you'll enjoy the game even more.

It seems that no golfer is immune to the trap of playing ahead of themselves. It's almost a natural tendency to worry about horrors lying several holes—even several shots—away. Architects design certain holes knowing that they'll get to you before you even play them. There are players in the Masters who worry on Tuesday about what they're going to play on Sunday!

Some players call it "planning ahead" when they obsess about future holes. There is such a thing as having a game plan, of course, and being reasonably prepared for what might happen later in the game. But if you let your worries get the better of you, it can end up being a self-fulfilling prophecy. If you play the game expecting bad things to happen, they just might.

Each moment in the game holds the possibility of being memorable. Paying attention to each moment as it comes, each challenge as it is offered, each hole as you play it, will allow you to play your best while enjoying the game most—and that is something worth remembering.

12.

Approach Each
Hole with a Game Plan

Playing golf without a game plan is like embarking on a trip without the slightest idea of how you're going to get to your destination. Lack of a well-thought-out game plan can be the source of a lack of confidence, bad moves, and a lot of worry.

If you go blindly into a game and fail to have your way at least somewhat mapped out, you'll end up swinging away without thought or concentration. The result of that, of course, can be disastrous, and only make you more upset. But if you've formulated a game plan before you hit the first tee, you can have an easier time visualizing your shots.

What goes into a good game plan? Decide which clubs you'll use, select your targets, and pick the best spot for your approach shot so that you optimize your putt. Taking these steps will help you play each hole with expectations of the route you want your ball to travel from the tee to the green and into the hole, stroke by stroke.

Plan with what you want to achieve in mind—to relax and have fun or really play well against your opponents, for instance. Your plan will give you a confident feeling that no matter what the game presents, you've thought things through and can deal with the expected and unexpected alike.

Once you make the plan, you must implement it, and most importantly, stick to it. Don't let emotions, positive or negative, cause you to toss your plan to the wind. Remember that you made the plan for a reason. If a chance to score presents itself, know when to gamble and take it and when to stick to the plan. Build some flexibility into your plan, as well, because course conditions can change even as you play. The purpose of making the plan is to play a relaxed, confident round, and use your head to put some discipline into your game. Your enjoyment of golf will increase greatly when you can play with confidence that you know what you're doing and where you're going.

13.
Practice Humility

It has been said that golf is the most humbling game of all games. It pays to remember that little statement on days when you're in the fortunate position of playing a really great game. A little humility can go a long way, especially if your partners aren't sharing in your good fortune.

It's okay to have a measure of confidence from your successes on the course, and in fact, you should. It will help you stay focused and can lead you to your best score. But if you display too much confidence, it can surely come back to bite you. Though you may love the game of golf dearly, accept that it can be extremely fickle. It behooves you to remember respect and humility when you're playing well. The game can turn quickly—with no warning, without rhyme or reason—and that can make any earlier displays of overconfidence seem intensely embarrassing. Additionally, conceit will weaken the impact of your accomplishments and inspire envy and resentment in others. Lack of humility is a sure way to ruin friendships on the golf course.

Every shot comes from the small place in between luck and skill. Understanding this can inspire humility and help prevent you from alienating others. Indeed, people are drawn to those who have no need to brag or steal the spotlight. You'll score much higher in the "human" category if you learn to share your good fortunes—both on and off the golf course—from your heart, and not from your ego. But your humility must be genuine, and developing that takes practice.

Learn to recognize the little signs that you might be ready to brag or behave in an overly confident manner. You can nip the behavior in the bud and enjoy your successes later, without bragging. Not only will others feel better about you, but you'll feel better about yourself. You'll also stand a much better chance of being invited to play with that group of people again, because humility will win out over ego anytime.

14.

Keep Your Perspective

If you're going to learn to do well on the course, it helps to keep your perspective. Then if you find yourself getting angry, irritated, or frustrated about something during your game, you'll be able to remember what's really important.

The concept is simple: Start by defining things that really matter to you. You may be surprised when you really think about it. Important things in life tend to be really important, like family emergencies, serious illness, death, divorce, substance abuse, bad accidents, being laid off at work, having your home burglarized, and so on. Think of as many of these situations as you can. When you consider situations of this nature, you come to realize that everything else really isn't that big of a deal. Does it surprise you that many of the things that you can get really worked up about on the course are really not so bad? It would be hard to place losing your ball in the woods in the same category as a serious traffic accident with injuries.

It's really that easy. Compare some of the other things that you personally thought were a big deal with things that really are, and see how quickly you'll put things into perspective. Somehow, a missed putt, a distraction during your backswing, or a bogey on the easiest hole on the course just don't come across as federal cases when you look at them this way.

The more you can keep your perspective, the better off you'll be, both in life and when playing golf. You'll discover that fewer things irritate you, and the word "play" will mean so much more every time you grab your clubs and head out to the course. You'll feel more relaxed and light-hearted, which will make others enjoy being around you, too. It can also help set the tone for your round, because just as bad feelings and low moods can be transmitted to others, so can good, peaceful feelings.

Arriving at the course with the idea that there's little worth stressing over is the most positive approach that a golfer can have—and that's likely to be a big boost for your game. As you play, any time that you find yourself losing your cool, remind yourself of what's really important in life, take a few deep breaths, and move on. You'll take the game in stride and keep right on playing—perhaps better than you'd been playing before.

15.

Become More Patient

Golf is a game that can quickly become ugly when players become impatient and frustrated. It can be a long five hours on the golf course if you or your partners are irritated and anxious throughout the game. The results can only be disastrous, particularly if you're playing with loved ones or business associates. Proper golf etiquette is the solution to this problem. Some of the etiquette rules may seem odd or "old-fashioned" to new golfers, but if you play the game long enough, you'll come to learn that respect for many of these rituals is also essential to the game.

Almost without exception, most excellent golfers practice all of the basic rules of etiquette. In fact, they're so practiced at proper etiquette that it seems to come naturally to them. Players who are impatient and display other awkward emotions, on the other hand, can stand out in the crowd, for such behavior goes against the basic rules of conduct, honor, and respect. Patience is the defining rule on the golf course. When you can be patient, you might discover that you can actually enjoy those moments of the game that used to frustrate you.

16.

Play Gratefully and Gracefully

Anyone who has spent time on a golf course playing the game knows that some days you've got it, and some days you don't. When you're playing well, you're on top of the world. Caught up in your happiness, you may even be self-congratulatory, possibly to the chagrin of your playing partners. But there are those days when nothing feels right, or you never have enough club, or just about every calamity on the course seems to befall you. Few things can make you feel worse than a partner who has got it that day and more or less rubs your nose in it.

The difference between golfers who have found balance with themselves and the game of golf and the ones who haven't can often be found in how they relate to their changing play. When you watch relaxed golfers who aren't worrying about little things, you'll likely see that when they're playing well, they're thankful that they are having a good game. Rather than bragging or flaunting their fortune, they are calmly grateful. They know how it feels to be on the receiving end of bragging. They also know that good days and bad days both pass, and that this will always be true as long as they can haul a bag of clubs from the first hole through the eighteenth. They understand that while they practice and strive for excellence, good play will come and go, and that some days they simply won't play as well. On those days, they are graceful in acceptance of their bad play.

Instead of becoming angry or complaining about course conditions or the weather, they know that this, too, shall pass. This may help them to look more objectively at their play and possibly find the reasons for their mistakes—if there are any. It may simply be that it's "one of those days," and if that's the case, graceful acceptance is all the more important to being relaxed and enjoying the game.

17.

Don't Blame
Other Things for Bad Shots

Few things can grate on golfers more than players who always blame their bad shots on something else. It's true that external elements may actually be involved in a bad shot, but even if that's the case, it's best to simply accept what happened and not look for excuses. This can go a long way toward easing tensions between you and your partners, as well as giving you a more positive outlook on your game as a whole.

You've probably played with someone who was pretty creative at finding reasons for a poor shot: "This slick grip made me slice the ball!" or, "I hooked it because you were moving during my backswing," or, "See, I told you that I'd top if I took your advice!" Anticipating the excuses that may pour forth from a partner's mouth can cause you stress before they even start, and the result will be that no one has much fun.

If this type of excuse-making sounds like you, however, you should think about possibly putting yourself into your partners' shoes for a moment and listen to yourself. Now imagine listening to that for the whole eighteen! There's nothing wrong with making some comments about your own bad hits every now and then, but there's a big difference between whining and complaining, and constructively analyzing why you may have hit badly. You can certainly ask your partners for some commentary, but the best thing to do is get off of the bad hit as quickly as possible and put your focus on your next shot, where it belongs.

Learning to accept bad shots as part of the game is another great example of learning to accept golf as a metaphor for life. Any time that you can surrender to the truth of the moment, even if that truth is a slice into someone's backyard, you'll become a more calm, peaceful person. Golf, just like life, won't always go the way that you want it to. When it does, you can be happy and grateful. When it doesn't, calmly accept what is, and do so without excuses. It's a much more powerful and positive way to live life and play golf.

18.

When in Doubt,

Let Someone Else Go First

The "honor" system can be confusing, and it sometimes leads to arguments among players. Honor defines whose turn it is to hit. It can get complicated when nothing is really cast in stone.

While you always want to follow the rules of etiquette and respect the honor system, sometimes it's less stressful to give up your honor. In fact, it can often be beneficial and work as part of your strategy. If you let someone else play first, no matter who actually has the honor, you can approach the game in a more positive way. For example, if you've earned the honor of going first because you made a birdie, you'll probably be very excited. The best strategy would be to settle down before you hit again. In this case, it would actually be nice not to have the honor. You can take the time to relax and ground yourself before your next shot. You know the feeling when you're playing well—your shoes stick to the turf and the tee. When you're not playing well, or if you're excited and distracted, you feel light as air and uneasy. If you can be still, regain your ground, and settle, you'll feel ready to hit. Passing on your honor can give you that time to settle down.

It's amazing how many golfers get pumped up and anxious so that they simply can't wait to go next. If you have that tendency, it can cause dissension in your group if you hit out of turn. You may then find that if you had waited, you would have been at a tactical advantage in your match. Learn to read yourself, and if there's a question of whose turn it is to hit, realize that it may be best to give up your honor.

19.

Agree with
Others' Assessments

All golfers have an opinion about not only their own play, but about how other golfers play. You may get frustrated with your own bad play and seek out the opinions of others, but then an interesting thing can happen. When you get an assessment of your bad play, you may disagree with it, argue with the person advising you, and become more stressed out than you were to start with.

This can be especially true in regular groups, where it can become a habit to critique each other's swings, and tips are offered whether you've asked for them or not. Rather than be defensive, say something like, "Okay, I'll have to remember that on the range." Using this tactic to deal with any unsolicited advice during the game can keep you calm. Your mental energy stays directed on your game.

Conversely, the criticism may be right on target. If that's the case, staying calm and agreeing with the critique can allow you to be open-minded enough to see the truth in the assessment. You may find that the other player has some good points, and this can lead to improvement on your part. But whether the assessment rings true or not, agreeing with it can keep you from becoming defensive.

The cold, hard truth is that your opponents may have ulterior motives when they offer tips. Golfers are crafty and can use criticism to their own advantage by upsetting an opponent and throwing her game. If you're actually looking for criticism, the best tactic is to wait for comments from a more impartial observer of your swing. Otherwise, take the assessments as they come, agree with them, and keep an open mind in case they're true. Everyone will be happier, and your game can keep going without disruption.

20.

Make Peace
with Slow Play

In an era when everyone is rushed and patience is limited, you may wonder that golf has sustained its popularity, considering how long it can take to play eighteen holes. It certainly says something for the strength of the game and the pleasure that millions derive from it.

However, we all reach a point where the time it takes to play eighteen holes coupled with the slow play of others can become a great irritation. It may even drive many from the game. There are faster alternatives to regulation eighteen-hole courses, such as par-3 courses, executive-length layouts, and nine-hole courses. Yet for some reason, many golfers will actually pass up the opportunity to play a faster round on a shorter, more enjoyable course.

On an eighteen-hole course, the slow play of others can make everyone's mood foul. Getting upset solves nothing. You need to distract your mind from the irritation and use the time to get into your mental game. At the height of his career, Jack Nicklaus would pass time by looking at the hole he was playing and thinking of ways that he would redesign it. Let's face it: Golfers tend to redesign holes that give them trouble. So instead of seeing a boring hole up ahead, use your extra time to try to make it more interesting. Be creative and put your mind anywhere but on how badly you want the foursome in front of you to get moving. You might also come up with ways to streamline your own play, thus moving the game along for those playing behind you.

Slow play is not a new problem, nor has the situation improved over the years. Therefore, it's best to accept it as yet another part of the game. The real solution, of course, is to slow down your life enough that a day on the course—even a long day—is relaxing and something you look forward to. Make golf your method of getting away from the other irritations of life. Slow down, relax, and get the most out of your favorite game at a good pace, without trying to hurry. You might find that your game, as well as your mood, will improve.

21.

Don't Let the
First Hole Ruin the Game

A common concern among golfers is playing the first hole. It's almost a superstition, as though what happens on the first hole is destined to happen throughout the round. Golfers allow the first hole to dictate the entire day. This doesn't have to be true, of course, but too often, players will lose their game because of a missed tee shot or missed putt on the first hole.

All it takes is an ugly tee shot out of bounds on that first hole, and you can end up saying to yourself, "It's going to be one of those days again." This can be a self-fulfilling prophecy, because you let the mistake irritate you. Your frustration and anger take away your focus and create tension in your swing. The "first-tee jitters" can also add to the problem. This is the nervous feeling that you get when you're about to hit your first shot of the day in front of everyone who's waiting to play the course. If you make a mistake, you think that everyone will notice.

Interestingly, doing exceptionally well on the first hole can also have a negative effect. If you happen to shoot a birdie, you now figure that you have to make every hole live up to the first one, and once again, you're so tense that you could bounce a quarter off of your biceps.

The way to establish a positive attitude and reduce tension for your whole game is to have a plan. Know what you're going to do on each hole so that if mistakes are made—even on the first hole—they won't affect you so much. You'll move on to the next hole feeling confident because you've thought the entire course through. Visualize yourself in a positive situation, and use that to maintain your pace. Don't forget to develop a consistent pre-shot routine, and use it from the first tee through the eighteenth green.

Getting off to a bad start doesn't have to ruin your game. It's a matter of planning, feeling confident, and knowing how to control your emotional highs and lows. Whether you're terrific or terrible on the first hole, take it in stride and remember that you've got seventeen more to go. Anything can happen!

22.

Stop Striving for
the "Perfect" Shot

One of the greatest sources of stress for a golfer is the idea that every shot should be perfect. It's true that you practice, analyze your swing, and learn as much as you can to improve your game. Every now and then, you're rewarded with a shot that can only be described as "perfect." Your tempo is smooth, your divot is just right, and the feeling of hitting the ball on the center of the club is solid. Whenever that happens, congratulations! The problem is that it's just not possible for every shot in every game to be absolutely perfect, no matter how hard you might try.

Having perfect shots as your goal will almost guarantee disappointment, frustration, and anger. Not every shot is going to go exactly where you've aimed it. When that happens, you've got two options: You can either analyze the situation, and make your next hit the best one you can make; or, you can get frustrated because the shot wasn't perfect, become tense and upset, and go on to possibly make an even worse shot. Which would you rather do?

The truth is that golf is a game of strategy, and that means thinking your game through. If you play with a well-thought-out game plan that's built on visualizing and going for your best shots, the chances of improving your score and really enjoying the game are significantly better. Chasing perfection can only lead to disappointment, because perfection is truly elusive. So why not make peace with imperfection? Strive to do your best instead of fighting an uphill battle for something that no one can achieve—not even the top pros.

23.

Trust Your Instincts

Golfers always have pieces of advice to give to other golfers. Giving advice is practically automatic. You're struggling with your long iron shots or your putting, and the suggestions pour forth from your partners. Most of the time, everyone means well, particularly if you're all good friends who are golfing for the fun of it and a little friendly competition. Because they mean well, you probably want to give their recommendations a try, even if you sometimes have trouble being open to learning from your friends. The problem is that trying to incorporate everyone's ideas into your play, whether they're right for you or not, will almost certainly ruin your game.

You can't always immediately identify which are the best ideas and which aren't. You may get caught up in trying so many different suggestions that none work due to your frustration level. In such cases, it pays to trust your first instinct regarding what advice to take and what to ignore. If your instinct is telling you that advice isn't accurate for you, then simply say to your friend, "Thanks, that's a good suggestion. I'll try that later." If you want to try it later, go ahead. But don't feel that you have to incorporate the idea into your game right that moment, and then feel guilty for not doing so.

You always want to remain open to suggestions from your friends and playing partners. In fact, sometimes you may want to ask them for ideas, particularly if you feel that someone knows the problems that you're working with and is pretty good at handling the same problem himself. Just be sure that you can sort through all of the unsolicited advice so that you don't wind up with information overload. You might end up swinging away with no plan at all and be worse off than you were to start with. That's when it's time to trust your instincts. If you just don't feel that a piece of advice is right for you, then it probably isn't.

24.

Leave Your
Complaints at Home

One thing that can turn a pleasant game of golf sour is a player who brings a cartload of complaints to the course. Golfers come to play with the intention of enjoying themselves, so don't bore your partners by complaining or listing your troubles. If you do it habitually, it may serve to come between you and your partners, and will certainly make the game less enjoyable for you.

It's especially tempting to bring up your troubles when your game isn't going so well. Your physical complaints can become explanations for a bad game: "My back hurts, so my swing is off today," or, "I can't focus on my putting, because bending over makes my neck hurt." While it may be true that the ache in your back is affecting your swing, you don't have to remind the world each time you make a shot.

If you're having a bad day, whether for health or other reasons, moodiness can ruin everyone's game. The truth is that if you're really feeling that badly physically or mentally, it's probably best to stay home and recuperate rather than aggravate the situation by trying to play. You can always play another day when you're feeling better and your mind is less occupied with problems. You'll be better company on the course, too.

It's completely possible to bear troubles and not let on to others. You can learn to accept your problems and irritations as a part of life, and then let go of the stranglehold that they have on your thoughts. If you don't break the cycle of obsessing about them, it leaves little room for the things in life you want to enjoy—like golf.

25.

Expect Bad
Bounces, Breaks, and Bunkers

Have you ever seen a golf course that didn't have bunkers, roughs, out of bounds, and water hazards? Of course not. These things are part of every golf course in existence, and they are there to challenge you and keep the game interesting. Naturally, your shots are going to hit the hazards sometimes, and you'll have bad bounces and breaks. But if you learn to expect these things when you golf, you won't be so frustrated when they happen.

Actually, you'd probably become extremely bored with golf if there were no bad breaks, lousy bounces, and various hazards. So if you come to expect these things every time that you play, you'll be less surprised, and therefore, less reactive when they happen. Instead of being angry when you lose a ball or frustrated when it plunks into the water, you'll simply feel like it's an aspect of the game. You'll take these things in stride, and your game will go a lot better because of it.

The best part of this strategy is that when you expect to run into these obstacles and don't, you'll be surprised on the positive side.

Understanding this strategy can help you to see that the majority of the time, you're probably playing quite nicely and your games do go smoothly. It's just that golfers tend to focus on the irritating and frustrating exceptions. You know that if you can't relax, focus yourself, and concentrate on each shot, you're just not going to play very well. So if you can reduce your stress and not be so affected by the bad breaks and bounces, you may even find that you'll have fewer bad breaks and bounces!

You don't have to learn to like the bad breaks and bounces—simply change your thinking to become more accepting when they do occur. When you can do this, you won't be tying your happiness to expectations that everything in golf—and life—will always go perfectly.

26.

Look for the Ordinary
in the Extraordinary

It's classic for golfers to obsess about unusual holes—signature holes, dramatic holes, or holes that have traditionally given them fits in the past. Maybe something odd tends to happen on these holes, or there's a design element that you just can't seem to conquer. When you approach these "obstacles," you might find yourself stressing over them instead of rising to meet the challenge.

There's a trick to dealing with these situations. Any time that your play takes a bizarre turn, think of a similar situation in the past and how you got out of it. The extraordinary circumstances that you find yourself in may not be so extraordinary after all. In golf, as in life, we tend to see what we want to see. If you search for the difficulties, frustrations, and things you "can't" seem to beat, that's exactly what you'll find. However, the opposite is true, as well. If you see extraordinary situations as "ordinary" by finding things that you're familiar with and have experienced before, you can deal with them in a much more relaxed manner. You can keep your game on track and your emotions in check.

One way to do this is to figure out a key phrase to say to yourself whenever you face a weird or wild situation. Use something that's reassuring to you and reminds you that you've gotten through these situations in the past. "I've been here before, okay? I can do this," is an example. The payoff in doing this is that no matter how strange the situation, if you can approach it in a relaxed and confident manner and can find something in it to relate to, it will trigger your imagination and let your creativity flow. You can visualize interesting shots and find ways to play the unusual elements by making them less daunting.

Try it and see if you don't find yourself actually looking forward to the extraordinary. It's all a matter of perception. If you perceive the extraordinary as strange and unconquerable, you'll have difficulty playing to the best of your ability. But if you see the ordinary in the extraordinary, you'll rise to the occasion and find far more enjoyment in the game of golf.

27.

Practice Makes Better,
but Don't Overdo It

There are those who think that hitting a lot of practice balls can be harmful, and that today's golfer practices too much without playing enough. However, if you practice without overdoing it, you can become a better player, and certainly a more relaxed and happier one. You can be inspired to try creative shots and to really involve yourself in your game.

The real beauty of practice is the door that it opens to beginners and those who don't have time to play a full round of golf. For the new player, a driving range is the perfect place to get over the initial battles with grip, stance, and fear. For those unwilling to commit to a full round because of cost and the length of time that it takes, a bucket of balls can be a relaxing experience and a wonderful way to take your mind off of other matters. Imagine how many people get through a day of unpleasant work with the knowledge they'll at least get to hit a quick bucket of balls later in the day. And how many times have you been down on your own game, only to experience a rejuvenation after a productive practice session?

Practice is also a nice way to tinker with your swing and really make significant improvements in your movement. There's little doubt that the importance now placed on practice is one reason that there are so many more good players today than there were just thirty years ago. But "productive" is the operative word when talking about practice sessions. Remember that too much practice, too much thinking, or just too much time on the range can hurt your game. You can get too technical, try too hard, and end up frustrating yourself. You can even develop bad habits if you don't limit your practice and make the most of it when you do practice.

Practice in the right measure, with the idea of enjoying yourself and being a better player, can keep new players coming to the game and let old golfers renew their passion for it when times get tough. The best attitude to develop about practice is the one described by Babe Zaharias: "Practice should be approached as just about the most pleasant recreation ever devised, besides being a necessary part of golf."

28.

Breathe
Before You Tee Off

How do you feel when you stand at the tee, ready to drive your first shot down the fairway? Many golfers approach their tee shots feeling tense and frustrated, most likely from previous holes, or even from a game the day before. Maybe they want to be like John Daly and take a long, hard swing at the ball. Their heads are filled with negative thoughts, and the result is often an overaggressive slash at the ball.

If this is the frame of mind that you sometimes find yourself in at the tee, you need to learn about the space between your thoughts. It's an interesting and unusual concept, but when you think about it, you'll see how it can help you calm down before you tee off.

There is a tiny space between your individual thoughts. It's really tiny, and you have to use your imagination to experience it. This space can be used as the key to setting your previous holes aside and clearing your mind to play the next hole. It's a moment of quiet amidst the noise of your thoughts. It's the moment when you have the choice to be nervous and uptight, or to take a deep breath and relax. It's like when you're about to say something but stop and change your mind. The space between your thoughts gives you a choice to either carry your negative thoughts and feelings over to your next hole, or put them aside and start fresh on the next tee. If you don't recognize this space right now, don't worry. Just being aware of its existence will allow you to begin finding it. The simple act of looking for it can slow you down and allow you to take that breath, breaking any negative or destructive chains of thoughts that you might have.

So the next time that you feel uptight as you're approaching your tee shot, take a moment to find the space between your thoughts. Then relax and take a deep breath before you drive, especially if your last hole wasn't up to par, so to speak. That moment to breathe before you tee off can make all the difference in the rest of your game.

29.

Learn the Lingo

We all want to feel as comfortable as possible playing golf, this most awkward and humbling of games. Knowing how to "talk golf" can be a big confidence booster, especially when the golf is more than just a leisure time activity. Most golfers can spot a novice or a non-student of the game right away, based solely on how that person refers to certain elements of the game. Knowing the differences between various terms can be fun, and is sure to lead to more enjoyable post-round banter.

Is the sandy hazard near the green called a "bunker" or a "sand trap"? Is the playing field known as the "links" or "golf course"? That pole stuck in the cup with a banner flying on it—"flagstick" or "pin"? Learning which terms traditionalists prefer to use and what is "correct" is part of the fun of the game. Besides, there's always at least one player at the golf club (not "country club") who relishes pointing out the misuse of terms by other players. Some pros can be quite insistent on using proper terms as part of playing the game correctly. Better to avoid the aggravation or potential embarrassment by taking time to learn the lingo and really become part of the family of golfers.

The amusing thing about the rhetoric of golf is that it's often viewed as insider's jargon, only open to ardent students or stuffy old rules officials. The truth is that understanding correct golf terminology is in everyone's best interest, from casual player to serious enthusiast. There's no disgrace in the ignorance of preferred golfing terms, however, because few golfers are ever properly introduced to the language and etiquette of the game. So get a jump on the others by taking time to learn the lingo. You'll find the game more enjoyable for it. (Incidentally, the traditionalists' choices from the list above are: bunker, golf course, and flagstick.)

30.

Do One Thing at a Time

It's easy to find examples of golfers doing too many things while trying to play. They yap on their cellular phones, shine their shoes, fret over where the beverage cart is, worry about the slightest noises that could distract their shots, and look for the course marshal to complain about a slow group. These golfers are all over the place, and so are their games. They make no attempt to tackle one thing at a time, and the one thing that they should concentrate on is playing the game.

Taking on too many things at once makes it impossible to keep yourself focused in the present moment. If you do that on the golf course, it's probably a habit that you're carrying over from other areas of your life. Let's face it: Our society is pretty hectic, and our culture revolves around gadgets and gizmos that are supposed to make it possible to do many things at once—as if that's a good thing. Thus we see people driving down the road, talking on cell phones, and eating fast food while scanning newspapers and listening to radios!

The dangers in this are fairly obvious. At home, you might watch TV, cook dinner, try to carry on a conversation with the kids, and feed the dog all at the same time. If you become used to this type of lifestyle, it's no wonder that you can't slow down, relax, and concentrate on one thing on the golf course.

You can fix this problem in all aspects of your life by consciously making the effort to focus on only one thing. What better place to start than on the golf course? Simply arrive at the course with the idea that all you're going to do is play golf, concentrating only on your game and being relaxed. You can leave your cell phone at home, get your beverages beforehand, stop worrying about your shoes (shoes get dirty, so get used to it), and leave the course marshal alone. Just play your game, and be in the moment. You'll probably notice that you really enjoy playing golf again. As a bonus, you just might be able to work out a few pesky little golf problems that you're having, because now you'll have your attention focused where it belongs.

Don't stop at the golf course. Practice doing one thing at a time in all aspects of your life. You might be amazed at how much more you'll get done by doing less all at one time. The only thing that it takes is a conscious decision on your part.

31.

Change Your Game
Plan as Needed

A lot of golfers play by the seats of their pants—they get to the course, jump right onto the first tee, pull out their clubs, and start swinging, without any forethought about the best way to approach the course. It's wise to have a game plan, to think out a strategy for how you want to play each hole. The best time to do that is prior to a round, and not while you're playing. Before the round, your mind is quiet and rational, so you can see your options and make good choices. But golfers who do make game plans often make the mistake of casting their plans in stone. No matter what happens, even if a plan is not working, they steadfastly refuse to deviate from it and make changes as they go.

Being inflexible can cost you. If you plan to hit down the left side of a hole, but suddenly find that the cup is on the right, in a place that you hadn't imagined, you would certainly do better to change your attack rather than stick with your plan.

Many players believe that they're choking if they make changes to their game plans. The truth is that you always need to be willing and ready to adapt to constantly changing conditions on the course and within yourself. You can't always know when the wind will come up, or if it will rain, or if your shoulder will start to hurt. When those things affect your game and your plan no longer works, don't keep right on following the plan in denial. Suppose you've been hitting a slice all day long—if you keep screwing the shot up, it's obviously not a productive plan to continue hitting it the same way. Changing your game plan based on what's happening at the moment may even save you a few strokes—or bring you out ahead. If your opponent hits a shot out of bounds, you can change your approach to be more conservative and win the hole.

It's usually beneficial to go with the flow and make changes to your plan rather than be frustrated. Flexibility in golf is an art. The pros practice it, but regular golfers rarely do. It's a sign of strength to evaluate a situation and be able to say, "I just don't have this shot today," or, "Okay, now I need to change," without feeling guilty or lousy about it. Though there are rules in golf that are set in stone, many other aspects of the game aren't, and your game plan is one of them. Rather than be frustrated, trust your own instincts, go with the flow, and change the plan if you find that it's not working for you.

32.

Dare to Play
the Tougher Route

Some avenues to the cup are more direct than others—that's part of strategic golf course design. But sometimes the more efficient ways can be a little tougher to negotiate. Let's face it: Good golf course design strategy is one of the primary reasons most people love to play golf. Some players, however, can view strategy as something to stress about. They avoid the challenges and take the "safe" route when they can. If you dare to play the tougher route, the reward for doing so successfully might be a putt for eagle or a better angle of approach to a well-bunkered green.

Course design strategy is the placement of hazards in a way that makes you think and gives you a choice of different avenues to "golf your ball" down to the hole, with some ways being more advantageous than others. Strategy is what ultimately separates great courses from not-so-good ones. Yet many golfers would rather be told how to play a hole, believing that anything requiring thought is strange and too complicated—or worse, something to complain and get irritated about. They expect one straight, fair, scenic route to a golf hole, and if they don't get it, they're unhappy with the course, and ultimately, their games. Such players may have a difficult time being satisfied on a well-designed course.

The truth is that good strategic holes make you think about what you have to do to conquer them. They make you contemplate the fun challenges of golf instead of the frightening hazards to avoid. Holes with no strategy (but with plenty of randomly placed hazards) make you think cautiously and often negatively, focusing more on what you can't do and must avoid, and that can stress you out. Plus it's just not very much fun.

Options, risks, mental dilemmas, decisions, intelligence, bravery —these are what strategy is all about. Good strategic holes give you the opportunity to be creative and challenge you to execute a variety of shots while still leaving open the possibility to play safely. They make you think of positive, creative approaches to the holes. For those who dare to take the tougher route and appreciate this wonderful aspect of the game, the enjoyment factor will be a lot higher, as well.

33.

Mind Your Own Game

Do you ever find yourself watching your playing partners closely and finding fault with every little move that they make? You might be thinking to yourself, "If I was her, I wouldn't play the hole that way," or, "How could he have possibly missed that shot?" or, "She really needs to keep her arm straighter if she wants that swing to improve." In fact, you may find yourself becoming irritated, bothered, and uptight by things that your partners are doing. You might even provide a nonstop stream of advice that may not be wanted or appreciated. Becoming so wrapped up in your partners' games makes it impossible to concentrate on your own.

Players may sometimes ask for your help or advice, and if that's the case, then feel free to oblige them. The trick here is to know when to lend advice or assistance and when to mind your own business. The truth is that unsolicited advice is rarely appreciated and often resented. You can ruin good player relationships by butting into others' games when you haven't been asked for help. You also open the door for others to start butting into your game, and then you'll understand firsthand why your advice isn't always desired.

Not minding your own game will inevitably lead to bad play on your part. Golf is a mental game as much as it is a physical one. If you don't give your own game the majority of your attention, your play will suffer, you'll become frustrated, and you won't enjoy playing. The result is that you'll be irritated, your partners will be irritated, and no one will reap the benefits of playing golf in the first place—relaxing and having fun.

Practice giving advice and counsel only when asked. This way, you won't be butting into anyone else's game when it's not appreciated. If you catch yourself butting in, simply back off. If you do, it's a good bet that everyone will have a much more pleasant and enjoyable game.

34.

Accept That
Luck Plays a Part

Just as in life, luck plays a far-ranging role in golf and will always be part of the game. It lends excitement to matches, and you'll never give up hope, because you know that there's always the chance that luck will intervene. If you do give up, it almost has to be because you haven't played long enough to see how luck can work its magic!

Luck is legitimately part of the real fun of playing golf. But sometimes players don't accept luck, preferring to have made all their good shots the "hard way." Preferring to be thought of as "skilled" players rather than "lucky," they actually take what luck gives them grudgingly. They believe that they "earn" good scores only with mastery of the game and not lucky breaks. You've probably seen such players—they brush aside congratulatory or complimentary remarks after a great hole or round, possibly becoming angry. Some even go so far as to say, "I didn't play that well—I was just lucky."

Of more concern to many golfers is their partners' luck. At the heart of dismissing luck as part of the game is the notion of absolute fairness. When competing, luck makes the playing field—or the course, in this case—uneven. You may appreciate a lucky break now and then, but only as long as it's yours and not your competitor's.

The truth is that luck happens, and we should be glad that it does. You can't stop it, so you may as well accept it in your play. Think of it as part of learning to go with the flow and accept "what is" in life. Rather than getting upset at a partner's luck or your own, see it for what it is: another essential element of the game. Embrace your lucky breaks and the lucky breaks of your partners. Without luck, the game of golf itself would suffer. Luck is part of the spirit of the game.

35.

Stick to the
Basics of Etiquette

Golf's rules of etiquette are full of subtleties and quirks. They will never make sense to a lot of us, but a few basics stand out as standards that every golfer must know in order to prevent tension or arguments from ruining a nice day on the links.

- Stand still and be quiet while others are playing. All other sports can have big, noisy crowds, so why do golfers need serenity? Because golf is a game that requires great concentration and allows little physical release. It's a game of precision, timing, and accuracy, with little room for mistakes.

- Mark your ball on the green unless it's your turn to putt. Not lifting and marking your ball is the sure sign of a novice. Gently urge such players to slap coins down behind those beat-up balls.

- Don't walk in someone else's line (the general direction toward the hole). This isn't difficult to grasp. When someone has a putt to the hole, don't step in his way. You probably won't mess up the putting surface if you do walk in his line, but it's a matter of respect more than anything else.

- Respect the "honor" system. If it's your turn to hit (your "honor"), then hit. If it's not your turn, don't hit. It's as simple as that. If your group is way behind the players in front of you, then you might suspend the honor system momentarily. But if you made a four on the last hole, and your opponent had a three, your opponent has "the honor" and should play first. And if she's farther away from the hole than you are, let her go first. It's not hard, but many anxious golfers can't wait and end up hitting out of turn, only to find out that if they'd waited, they would have been at a tactical advantage in their matches.

Some quick reminders: Hole all of your putts without asking, "Is this good?" (This is a guaranteed friendship-killer if your partner doesn't want to concede the putt.) Use no more than fourteen clubs—the maximum as spelled out in the rules of golf. Play the ball as it lies (unless the course has deemed conditions to be winter rules). Help your playing partners search for their lost balls. Most of all, try your best to respect the rules of golf. Even if you and your friends are just out for fresh air, it's still important to play by the rules. Your playing partners and your little inner voice will feel a whole lot better about you, even if you think no one notices that you're adhering to the rules.

36.
Let Your
Kids Caddie

In the good old days, kids and young adults would carry clubs for a small fee and could make good money caddying over the summer months. Byron Nelson and Ben Hogan both fell in love with the game while caddying as young boys at Glen Garden Country Club in Texas, and both referred to those days as their inspiration to pursue careers in golf. There is no better way to play golf than to walk and have your clubs carried by a quiet, hardworking, devoted caddie.

Few kids get the opportunity to caddie today, but if you're lucky enough to play at a club that allows caddies, be sure to give your kids the chance to caddie for you and others. It builds their self-esteem, and it means a lot for kids to feel included with the adults. Not only that, it's a simple way to introduce a young man or woman to golf. Many adults learned the game as kids, caddying for their parents and grandparents and perhaps hitting a few balls with them every now and then.

For the kids, there are many benefits. Caddying exposes young people to the game, the rules, the etiquette, and all of the little elements that aren't always easy to pick up, but which can be learned quickly on the course while watching others. It's a bonus if they're getting paid to do so, as well. As caddies, young people watch their elders play golf and observe how they behave. Watching an adult throw a golf-related tantrum can do amazing things for young people. They can see the foolishness of the behavior and are less likely to act in such a way when they play golf. In fact, adults can benefit from having kids as caddies, too. Adults will behave better, play by the rules, and practice etiquette because they know that kids are watching them.

Imaging how rewarding it can be to kids when adults actually ask them for advice. Even if it's just to make a decision between a 5- or a 6-iron, the slightest bit of success that comes from their advice provides an emotional lift to them that's immeasurable.

If your club has a caddie program, by all means, let your kids take advantage of it. They can get right in on the action and learn about the game, and you can spend more quality time together, too.

37.

Look for Incremental
Improvement

Sometimes, you may feel that all the practice, game analysis, advice, and lessons in the world aren't doing a thing to improve your game. You have a feeling of being stuck and not moving forward. This can be frustrating to the point where you become overwhelmed trying to fix your swing or cure your slice. At times like this, you need to step back a bit and try to see yourself from a different perspective. We're often too close to our own golfing experiences to see the little changes that do take place when we're committed to practicing.

This is a problem of expectations, and the key to this strategy is to stop expecting perfection from yourself. First you have to realize that you won't become perfect overnight and, in fact, you probably won't ever become perfect. Once you accept this, you can begin to look for the little, incremental improvements in your game. If you really take time to look, you'll probably find them. You may have an ongoing problem with swinging "over the top," but you might find on closer inspection that the problem really isn't quite as bad as it used to be. When your focus is narrowed to see only the problem itself, you can sometimes block out the fact that you really are making progress a little bit at a time.

Do you tend to seek perfection in other areas of your life, as well? Doing this on the golf course could be part of a larger problem—you may find on close inspection that you expect similar perfection in your home or work life. Seeking perfection in life only sets you up for disappointment, because in real life there is always going to be imperfection. If you accept this and learn to look for incremental improvement, both at home and on the course, you'll feel less stressed and find a great deal more joy in life.

38.

Respect
the Short Par-3s

A golf architect once built a short but scary par-3 for a new private course. It was an old style, do-or-die hole that at ninety-seven yards was obviously reachable for everyone who played the course. But a particularly boisterous potential club member tried to convince others not to join this new club because, he pronounced, no respectable championship-quality course should have such an absurdly short hole. Sadly, many players listened to his reasoning.

Many players get caught up in obsessing about the numbers in golf—not just the score or which club to use, but par and hole length. They view the short par-3s, and sometimes even par-4s, as less than challenging. They believe that short holes require less skill and are not worth their time.

Such holes aren't all as easy as you might think. These are often the holes that require the most thought. In fact, Ben Crenshaw has said that such holes are "one of the many ways to check unbridled power and occasionally, make those long hitters' knees tremble." Par-3 holes can be really fun to play and exciting to our senses. Rather than complaining about them or snubbing courses that have them, you should make the most of them.

How? By focusing on your mental game. Though a hole may be short, the architect will often throw in little elements to make it trickier and more strategic. From time to time, Joe Golfer can even beat Larry Tourpro on a short par-3. All it requires is that he place his ball on the right portion of the green. If he does that, a birdie becomes possible, making the par-3 hole a place where something interesting and sometimes humbling occurs. Short holes give lesser players an occasional—and necessary—ray of hope, and provide them an opportunity to show the better players that it pays to have finesse, skill, and courage.

Holes under 140 yards are great equalizers. Young and old players, long and short hitters, all have the same vantage on the tee. That's what the spirit of golf is all about—everyone having fun, playing to their own satisfaction, and enjoying the game.

39.

Understand That
Golf Isn't Always Fair

On the golf course, as in life, we sometimes expect total and complete fairness. Players often get so caught up in controversy over the supposed lack of fairness of golf that they may even quit the game. But they miss the point that golf is better because it isn't fair, and in fact, it was never intended to be fair. Surrendering to that fact can encourage you to do the very best that you can on any course and allow you to enjoy the game, no matter what twists and turns it takes.

Those who wish that the game were fair push hard for course designs that are equalizing. But too often, the majority of design features are developed in the name of fairness, making the game less challenging for some and downright boring for many. In an effort to speed up play, many exciting holes may be stripped of their features before architects, developers, committees, and municipalities realize that golfers are slow, no matter what they do!

Sadly, the fairness mindset has even caused many older, once-classic course designs to be modified. On courses by MacKenzie, Ross, and Tillinghast, bunkers have actually been filled in because they supposedly punished the average player and served no purpose for the good player. The truth is that those bunkers weren't placed to punish the average golfer. Rather they were designed to make the game more interesting for the average player, to make holes look harder than they really were, and to give the average golfer something challenging yet achievable to cope with. Removing these elements, particularly in the name of fairness, lessens the game considerably.

Golf is supposed to be fun, and yes, sometimes it's unfair. But if golfers keep demanding that everything perceived as unfair be eliminated, they're going to be left with boring courses, and worse, a sport of little challenge and variety. When you accept that golf isn't fair, you'll complain less, spend more time working to become a better player and partner, and stick with the game, even when the playing gets tough.

40.

Become a
Less Aggressive Driver

What shot tends to make you the most uptight during your round? A lot of golfers put tee shots high on their list, often over putting. If your last hole didn't go as well as you might have liked, or your putt was less than stellar, the tee shot on the next hole can be seen as a chance to redeem yourself, not just in your own eyes but in those of your partners. You can put a lot of pressure on yourself to perform on that tee shot.

The result of that self-imposed pressure can be a tendency to pull out and drive as hard as you can. This can lead to a slice, a topped shot, a nasty hook, or even the dreaded whiff—every possibility except a well-struck, productive tee shot. What you really need to do is slow down, quiet yourself, and become a less aggressive driver. There's nothing wrong with approaching the tee assertively and with confidence, but replacing muscle and hard hitting with finesse and calm can land your ball in the fairway. When you become a less aggressive driver, you do several things. You leave the previous hole behind, eliminating a need for redemption. You quiet your mind not only between shots, but between holes. And you try to read the hole, to figure out what the course designer created. Using your head to try to outsmart the designer will get you a lot farther, literally and figuratively.

The tee shot sets the mood and feel for the entire hole—"bad tee shot, bad hole" is a common way to think. The aggressive driver who makes mistakes can certainly set himself up for a disappointing hole. But that only happens if you let it. Instead, throttle back and approach the drive gently. You'll stand less of a chance of ruining your shot, thereby setting up a better feeling for the rest of the hole.

Remember, there's no need to smash, overpower, or overdrive the ball. You can end up in a myriad of bad places if you don't take it slow and easy. Becoming a less aggressive driver is more about how to attack the course than the ball. This is a strategy that you can use to your advantage for years to come.

41.

Accept That You
Can't Truly Understand "Par"

What is "par"? The word itself can send shudders through golfers who strive so hard to shoot under it but instead go well over it. The distinguished writer Charles Price said of par: "Tell somebody on the golf course you're under par and he'll envy you—tell somebody off the golf course you are under par and he'll feel sorry for you. Is it any wonder that golf's the game where the lowest score is the best score?"

Par is from the Latin word "par," meaning "one that is equal." That doesn't tell you much when discussing par and golf, particularly when you try to explain that a 175-yard hole and a 250-yard hole can both be a par-3. Par has to do with the degree of difficulty in playing the hole, of course, but that makes the determination of par—and its true meaning—even more complicated.

The idea that par is the standard for great play is one of the more peculiar myths of modern golf. The game is at a point where if anyone shoots well below par, it means that something went wrong. Low scores posted by tour pros have come to mean to most observers that the course has defects, or that the players really weren't properly tested. Yet other sports rarely question achievement when it occurs. In track and field, do we question the quality of the surface if a runner breaks a world record? No, it's felt to be a remarkable human achievement, not a fault with the facility.

Recreational golfers obsess about par, yet most professional players never state their scores in terms of par. This takes the pressure and stress off right away. Rather than saying that you shot "five over par," simply say that your score was "77." The fact is that virtually no one really understands par. It's a liberating feeling to stop making yourself a slave to par and simply play the game because you enjoy it, not to chase a number.

42.

Let Go of Your
Expectations on the Course

Everyone has days when things on the course turn out much differently than expected. Maybe the sun is shining when you leave home, but by the time you get to the club, it's gray and drizzling. You feel good at the beginning of your warm-up, but suddenly your swing feels awkward or your back stiffens. A new playing partner turns out to be a nonstop talker, which makes you tense. The greens are aerated and sandy. And your game plan? You're ready to toss it on the third hole! Even your favorite holes disappoint you: You expect an easy drive on the ninth, but you top your tee shot. Your score is the final proof. On a day like this, you feel like you shouldn't have gotten out of bed, let alone put golf clubs in your hands.

Although we often wish it to be perfect, life rarely turns out the way we expect. Golf also functions like this. We expect to drive well on certain holes and putt well on others. We expect the greens to be cut a particular way, or to play the round in a reasonable four hours.

We may even expect our partners to behave a certain way. When things turn out differently, we're disappointed and may become upset or angry. We blame others for our frustrations, and fail to see that we play a big part in it by having high expectations in the first place.

Think about it: If you expect your partners to like a new layout that you're playing, but it turns out that they aren't thrilled with the course, you may feel disappointed. But if you allow for the fact that others may not share your enthusiasm for a particular course, or a certain brand of golf ball, or even which day of the week to play on, then you can let disappointment roll off your back. This is true for your game, too. You can't expect to strike each chip shot perfectly, to make every short putt, or to drive that ball straight down the fairway on every hole. If you do, you'll certainly be dissatisfied with the game of golf and let the little things get you down.

Letting up on expectations will reduce your stress when things don't go your way. This isn't to say that you should lower your standards or give up your preferences. As a golfer, you should always strive to improve and play the best game you can. It simply means that you should be more open to the things that spontaneously occur in life and on the golf course, and more willing to accept them. It's a more peaceful way of living and approaching your game, and you'll feel a lot happier when you can put it into practice.

43.

We All
Make Mistakes

No one's perfect, least of all a golfer. More than any other sport, golf is a game of good misses as much as it's a game of precision play. Ben Hogan and Jack Nicklaus have said that a fine day would be one in which they hit seven or eight shots the way that they wanted to, and most good golfers would agree. Golf is a hard game, and we can't all be perfect players.

It does no good to make a big deal out of your mistakes on the course. But you can use them to learn, grow, and improve your game. The true problem comes from being unwilling to either acknowledge or examine the mistakes that you make, thus leading to a tendency to repeat them. We all make mistakes in life. If we were discouraged from trying to correct our errors, life wouldn't be much fun. Nor would golf, if we always had to chip out sideways instead of occasionally trying for the heroic slice around a tree and onto the green. If we never got a chance to recover, few of us would pursue life or golf with zest.

The real joy of golf lies in the many opportunities for redemption. Even after some of your worst shots, you might still have hope of finding your ball and hitting a daring recovery shot. A recovery shot pulled off in dire circumstances requires imagination, bravery, and great skill. Take a look at your own mistakes. The fact that you made them is no big deal, but how you handle the mistakes is what really makes or breaks your game.

Noted golf writer and architect Robert Hunter has said: "The keenest delight in golf is given to those who, finding themselves in trouble, refuse to be depressed, and, with some recovery, snatch from their opponents what seemed for them certain victory." Accept that mistakes are part of the game—you'll no longer feel that recovery shots are impossible, and you may actually begin to believe that they're highly probable.

44.

Tolerate
the Soft Spikes

Golfers have taken to complaining about "soft spikes," those plastic knobs screwed into the soles of your golf shoes that can be a real irritant to players, but are good for the course. Soft spikes came about in the mid-1990s to replace regular golf spikes. Problems with players dragging their feet and tearing up the greens became widespread and no longer tolerable by most golf course superintendents. Soft spikes cut down on such damage.

Soft spikes, however, are not as safe for golfers as metal spikes. They don't give you as much traction, making slipping on wet surfaces a hazard. Taking a full swing on the tee can be problematic when your shoes don't give you the control that you need. If a player slips while teeing off, it certainly will tee her off.

If a course requires soft spikes, don't get agitated. Simply think about the extra precautions that you need to take. You'll sink more putts because the green isn't all torn up by their metal counterparts.

45.

Count to Ten
at Tree Roots

Who doesn't love a beautiful tree? Few things in nature are more appealing or remarkable than a stately, 200-year-old tree. Trees hold a special place in our hearts because they're living, breathing plants that take root in the ground and manage to survive some of nature's harshest assaults. However, as much as we may love them, trees on a golf course seem to be regarded as the ultimate hazard, more so than bunkers, creeks, or interesting little undulations. They do pose some problems if your ball happens to land in the proximity of a thick, knotty tree root, or worse, a system of roots. Unfortunately, under the current Rules of Golf, you can't get relief from tree roots.

Many golfers fail to stop and think about their options when their balls are among roots. Rather than take a drop or a one-stroke penalty, a frustrated golfer may simply swing away, rushing to get out of the tangle quickly and get back to business. That approach holds the danger of injured wrists. To avoid the possibility of injury, it's best to take a deep breath, count to ten, and really examine your options. If you do, you'll either find a good, safe shot out of the roots, or realize that you have to take the penalty and move on. If that's the case, bite the bullet, take the drop, and don't obsess about the roots and that extra stroke for the rest of the round.

Golf can be a very difficult game, and it's hard enough when you have an 8-iron in your hand, a great lie, and a small bunker to carry over. As lovely as they are, trees introduce an element in golf that can be awkward, difficult, and bizarre, to say the least. Take some comfort in the fact that trees provide for some exciting recovery shots from time to time. But when you find yourself in an impenetrable forest, don't let tree roots cause slow play or take the fun out of your round. Count to ten, and make a wise, safe decision. Then remember those roots when you make your next game plan.

46.

Use Your
Imagination—Carefully

Nothing in golf provides more irony than your own imagination. Possessing a vivid imagination can compensate for various mechanical and physical shortcomings, and can salvage rounds that would otherwise have been disastrous. On the other hand, possessing an intense imagination can quickly become a golfer's worst enemy. The ability to envision creative and original shots while also having enough control to avoid looking for trouble can lead you to great success. Using your imagination to focus on the simplest route to the hole is vital to success in golf.

Imagination is fascinating in the way it can, at times, be oblivious to meddlesome out-of-bounds stakes or lakes blocking your way to the green. At other times, your brain can't seem focus on anything but a particular hazard, or harbor dreadful suspicions that you're going to hit a wild slice into someone's backyard. The trick is to maintain creativity and the ability to manufacture stroke-saving shots without allowing your imagination to lead you astray. Pre-shot, positive visualization can be the key, and it really does work for many players. Some of the best players do it consciously; others do it without realizing it. Jack Nicklaus was spectacular at it.

Golf will always require players to use their creative instincts to master a course. Creative players who can work their way around a strategically designed course without losing control of their thoughts will stand out. So before you hit a shot, close your eyes, relax, take a few breaths, and see the shot that you want to hit. Visualize the ball taking the path that you think will work best, and then see it finish the way you want it to finish. That is when imagination will serve you best.

47.

Quiet Your Mind
Between Shots

You've seen golfers who try to play a round at the highest possible level of focus for six hours or more. They know that just one poorly planned and executed shot could ruin their whole game. Between shots, they immediately worry about the next shot, or perhaps even the next hole. It's stressful just thinking about it.

With the average round taking longer than ever, it's hard to expect anyone to maintain absolute focus over the course of five or six hours. Unwavering concentration is ideal for great golf, and it's present on those days when we're in the zone. But the best players know how to concentrate on the shot at hand, and then quiet their thoughts in between shots. They keep themselves fresh and don't suffer from burnout at the end of a round. In fact, the best players seem to have a remarkable talent for leaving their poor shots behind them. They also avoid dwelling on dilemmas looming in the near future. They practice being in the present moment.

How can you keep your mind in the present when there's so much time on the course to consider the possibilities? Deep breathing, visualization, practicing meditation, and playing regularly can all help. In between shots, close your eyes and focus on your breathing, in and out. Open your eyes, and if thoughts of the previous shot—or worries about the next shot—enter your mind, gently let them go and bring your focus back to your breath. Practice this method of clearing your mind while moving on to your next shot. Concentrate on the rhythms of your body every time that you play, and soon it will become one of your regular habits, just like steadying your stance or marking your ball.

It takes some practice, but the results can be well worth the effort. A quiet mind will bring you inner and outer peace. This can be a remarkable tool on the golf course, when being calm and steady can make the difference between a nasty slice and a well-struck shot down the middle, or between a confidently struck putt and the yips.

48.

Lighten Up
Your Pre-Shot Routine

Pre-shot routines are those familiar little rituals that can become like a security blanket for players. They can help you get into that mysterious level of comfort and focus commonly referred to as the "zone," no matter where you're playing or who you're playing with. But a long and tedious pre-shot routine involving a lot of practice swings, perfectly timed waggles, false starts, and lining up the shot over and over are sure to frustrate not only your partners, but the foursome behind you.

You probably know at least one golfer who is a devotee of the mental game of golf and has crafted a precise, nine-part pre-shot routine. You may go to lengths to avoid being in a foursome with this player, and that's understandable. The trick to a good pre-shot routine that won't offend others is to do it economically, and only to remind you of whatever it is that gives you the most comfort in your swing. You may need a slow practice swing to remind you of tempo, or you may need to select something small to aim at in order to prevent alignment errors. You and your teacher know your game best. There's little doubt that a simple routine will improve your consistency if you can follow it.

It's okay to stand behind the ball, visualize the shot, put your glove on, and even wiggle a few times—whatever makes you comfortable. When all is said and done, we play the game for fun. We play golf to enjoy the company of others and to spend time outdoors in a beautiful setting. More power to you if you can develop a pre-shot routine that gets you into the zone from time to time and helps control your imagination the rest of the time. Once you find what helps you, then work to tighten it up and lighten it up. Keep it simple and short, for the sake of your partners and those behind you.

49.

Be Grateful for
the Occasional Flyer Lie

Golf is full of elusive mysteries that make it adventurous and exciting. The most peculiar and hard-to-explain mystery of golf is the flyer.

Most golfers consider this mystery to be a gift if they get one. A flyer is when your ball lies in semi-long rough, and just enough grass blades nestle themselves between your ball and your clubface that when you hit the ball, something amazing can happen. Sometimes at impact, the grass blades conspire with your clubface to send your ball unbelievably long distances. It doesn't always happen, and there's no way of actually knowing when a flyer will occur, though usually it's when you can make good contact with the ball.

The flyer lie poses mental challenges and strategic dilemmas to a good golfer. It rewards those who can understand the art of judging a flyer and gives them an excellent chance to show off their talents. Luck goes hand in hand with the flyer lie, particularly if you happen to find one in the middle of the fairway. But remember that luck is simply part of the game, so take your lucky breaks when you can get them. The joy of reading a flyer lie correctly and making it work is something that you can remember when your game isn't going so well. It will help you stay positive and get your game back on track.

The flyer is an elusive mystery of golf, and it adds an interesting element, as long as it doesn't happen all the time. That would be too much of a good thing, even in golf.

50.

Give Up the Cart

It would be beneficial for most golfers if they gave up the cart once in a while. There are many who believe that widespread use of carts has driven up the cost of course maintenance because of the damage that they inflict. Others say that golf courses can be impossible to walk on if they're designed with cart use in mind, and some players simply don't like unsightly cart paths in the natural beauty of golf courses.

The truth is that carts eliminate half of the reason that most golfers are out there in the first place: to get some good exercise while enjoying the game. With that in mind, it's sad to see that many young golfers who are able to walk are choosing instead to rent carts. That's not to say that carts are always bad and should be eliminated, however. If used appropriately, carts have a place in the game for those who wouldn't be able to play if they weren't able to ride between shots. Many older people and disabled people get to play because they can take carts. Thus carts put golf within reach of more people. While carts can be the cause of increased maintenance, they can also be the source of increased revenue to pay for that maintenance and more, and everyone wins in that case.

So for traditionalists who hate golf carts, remember those who would not be able to play if it weren't for four wheels. For those of you who can walk or who can afford a caddie, leave the carts for those who need them. Give up the cart at least once in a while, and walk the course for fun and your health. You may even see aspects of nature and your home course that you never noticed when you were zooming around in that little buggy.

51.

Practice Patience

Golf requires bucketloads of patience to play and to practice. Interestingly, you don't have to be born with a patient personality to develop the quality of patience. You can work deliberately to develop it and actually practice patience.

Think of patience as an art form. You can create actual patience practice periods, or better yet, incorporate patience practice into your golf practice. Here's how: You know what problems in your game are bothering you, and they're what you work on in practice. Before you start, make the conscious decision to remain patient and say to yourself, "While I'm driving this bucket of balls, I won't let anything bother me. I'll be patient." Something quite interesting may then occur. When you approach patience deliberately, your capacity to be patient is increased. Patience is also one of those things that can build on its own success—if you can be patient through that bucket of balls, you may find that you can be patient through the next one, and the next. The trick is to recognize situations where you may tend to lose your patience, and specifically work on being patient at those times.

The golf course is your classroom when it comes to learning patience. A round of golf can take four or five hours. One must think a shot through, wait for slow players ahead, deal with distractions, plan putts, and search for lost balls. Each of these situations presents a challenge to be patient, and with each one, the rewards for becoming more patient can be great. Instead of giving you high blood pressure and stress, patience lets you deal with your game problems—and people problems—in a calm manner. That's the best way to fully enjoy the game of golf.

52.

Don't Overdo
the High-Tech Gear

Anything that makes golf more enjoyable and easier for average players should be applauded. It's great when people have fun and keep coming back to play what can be a frustrating and difficult game. If a new driver or new putter is the ticket to keeping players interested, then so be it. But the typical golfer can overdo the high-tech gear, spending a lot of money to acquire equipment that won't necessarily improve his play or enjoyment of the game.

You probably have little need for the latest $500 driver, your third new set of irons in three years, or a graphite-shafted putter. You may get some enjoyment out of it, and if that's enough for you, then indulge. But before you start amassing a collection of trendy but mostly useless items, ask yourself a few questions: "Do I really need this?" "Will it help improve my game?" "Can I afford this?" "Do I want it just because it's the latest thing?" Reflect on your answers to those questions before you open your checkbook or slap down that credit card.

The real problem here is that your need for golfing gear can become insatiable and never-ending. Once you get an item that you want, that fulfilled desire is immediately replaced by the desire for something else. In this cycle with no end, you're never happy with what you have, and nothing you get can make you happy. And don't forget the real issue here—what you're obtaining may not be doing a thing for your game. Clothes, equipment, training videos, books, lessons—none of these may make a bit of difference if they don't help, and you're not going to be happy.

It's better to make do with what you have, rather than constantly wanting something else. The anxiety and frustration of always "needing" and wanting more can ruin the whole game for you. Why not make the decision to put a ceiling on your desires and stick to the real basics? Play the old-fashioned way and enjoy it—you'll save money, too.

53.

See the Forest
for the Trees

A lot of golfers think that there are too many trees on golf courses. In fact, many believe that trees belong on a golf course about as much as they do in the middle of a football field or right behind the pitcher's mound of a baseball diamond. Many players can be thrown into a state of anxiety at the sight of a lone tree placed down the center of the fairway, and ruin their games because of it. But you can learn to "see the forest for the trees" and keep them from bothering you. This means to see the trees not as obstacles out to get you on the course, but as nature's elements that can actually be used to calm and focus you. For those who suffer tree anxiety, this strategy can be very effective.

It's easy to see how focusing on the negative aspects of trees can cause you to worry about their presence. Trees were not part of the first golf courses, but today, they're used as a major design element on many courses. Trees can hinder your ability to find your golf ball and play it. Roots can cause you to lose strokes. Trees have even been used in golf course trickery, as in 1979, when a full-grown tree was transplanted overnight to block a shortcut to a hole during the U.S. Open at Inverness.

You can learn to look at trees in a positive way, however, if you learn to shift your attitude to see trees as simply being there. Suppose you have a busy mind that can't focus. You can relax by looking at the trees and using them as a tool to zone out. Focus on the trees to calm down between shots or holes. Remember, too, that trees can provide for some exciting recovery shots from time to time. You've seen wild slices into the trees redeemed by valiant and memorable recoveries. Think of trees as one more thing to add variety to your game.

Golfers can probably agree that a few trees are nice, as long as they don't cramp your play or block lovely vistas. Used judiciously, trees can enhance the beauty of golf courses and act as safety buffers between fairways. Trees can occasionally be placed to add interest or beauty to a hole. But if they're placed where they distract you, learn to change your thinking. See the forest for the trees, and you'll enjoy a more relaxed round.

54.

Embrace the
Humor of Golf

You know that you're having a bad day on the course when someone tells you that you'd better hurry up and take your shot—and you already have. The problem is that the ball ended up so close to you that the other person couldn't tell. Okay, so it's an old joke that unfortunately has actually happened to you, and it wasn't funny then, either. But you have to admit that golf holds so much potential for humor that sometimes you can't help but laugh at the game—and at yourself. At least you should be able to laugh. If you ever find yourself taking the game of golf too seriously, consider embracing the humor of the game, as these famous folks did.

"It's good sportsmanship not to pick up lost balls while they are still rolling." —Mark Twain

"The only shots you can be dead sure of are those you've had already." —Byron Nelson

"I'm in the woods so much, I can tell you which plants are edible."
—Lee Trevino

"Golf's a hard game to figure. One day you'll go out and slice it and shank it, hit into all the traps and miss every green. The next day you go out and, for no reason at all, you really stink." —Bob Hope

"Golf is a game in which you yell 'fore,' shoot six, and write down five." —Paul Harvey

"Golf is a game whose aim it is to hit a very small ball into an even smaller hole with weapons singularly ill-designed for the purpose." —Winston Churchill

"My game is so bad I gotta hire three caddies. One to walk the left rough. One for the right and one for the middle. And the one in the middle doesn't have much to do." —Dave Hill

55.

Get Over the
Previous Hole

Just as few golfers are immune to the trap of playing ahead of themselves, we all can get into the habit of carrying frustrations with us from a previous hole. This can make it difficult, if not impossible, to relax and concentrate on the hole that we're playing. You can see how your entire round can be ruined with excess baggage. The idea of playing the course one hole at a time becomes quite important in this case.

There was a Zen master who once said that life is "one mistake after another." It wouldn't be surprising to hear that this guy also played golf. Once again, golf imitates life. As we go through life from day to day, making mistakes, fixing them, learning from them, and changing, we do the same in golf, too. If you look at the triple bogeys, the mishits, and the stupid decisions as opportunities to learn, it's easier to forgive yourself and move past the mistakes. You don't entirely forget them, of course. You want to work on your problems when you practice. And if you really want to put your mistakes into perspective the next time that you try to hit a straight drive, remember that Babe Ruth struck out twice for every home run that he hit. That's something to think about whenever you could use a ray of hope.

Take some time between holes to relax your muscles, quiet your mind, and forgive yourself for any bad hits you may have just had. Maybe the entire hole was something you'd rather forget. As you proceed to the next hole, leave the mess behind and get over that hole. The past is past. You'll learn, make the necessary adjustments, and move on. Remember to play the hole that you're on, and you may even realize that the previous hole is nothing to waste your energy thinking about.

56.

You Can't Always
Play Your "A" Game

There's no doubt that when you're playing your "A" game, you're on top of the world. That's your best game, of course, when you seem to do everything right. It's when you swing gracefully, play intelligently, and have touch on and around the greens. But you can't always play your "A" game. You'll have good days and bad days, and it does you no good to become stressed and angry whenever you're having an off day. When you're not playing at your best, accept it and take the time to learn from the experience.

Most pros take the mental approach that they're rarely going to hit the shots that they want, and will probably hit only a few "perfect" shots a round. They don't actually go into a round or a tournament expecting bad things to happen. Instead, they don't expect perfection, and therefore aren't surprised when they aren't perfect. They have it in mind that if bad things do happen, it's part of the game and they'll learn something from it. Many pros truly believe that if they can hit seven or eight shots the way that they want to in a game, that's a terrific day.

If you really pay attention the next time that you watch a pro tournament, you'll see that the best players only hit a few good shots in every round. So it's unrealistic to think that you'll be playing your "A" game every time you go to the course. If you can develop this attitude and not expect to play your "A" game every time, you won't be so hard on yourself if you hit only one or two good shots.

It's a great day when you play your "A" game, but you just won't do it every time. Don't expect the worst, or you just might get it. Simply accept that you're not perfect, just like everyone else on the course, including the pros.

57.

Get Your Game
Off to a Peaceful Start

A good way to set the tone for your round of golf is to arrive at the course with a game plan and a calm, peaceful mind—but that doesn't always happen. Sometimes, you can let your thoughts get away from you and arrive at the course feeling uptight and tense. If you don't calm your mind and feel good when you get there, it's a recipe for bad hits and possibly a miserable round.

Think about this scenario: You're looking forward to playing, but your round last weekend didn't go so well. On the first hole, you hooked your tee shot into the cart barn. On the eighth, you hooked another shot even worse into the woods. Then you really blew it on the twelfth, hitting that same wicked hook into the lake. As you go through this in your mind on the morning of your game, you find yourself becoming apprehensive about playing that twelfth hole again. Your little mistake on the eighth comes back to you, and now you're even getting worried about the first hole. By the

123

time you're ready to walk out the door, you're a mental wreck—and you haven't even left home yet! Imagine what your mental condition might be by the time you arrive at the course. If your warm-up doesn't go well, you certainly figure that your game is doomed. Not exactly the most peaceful way to start a round, is it?

Rather than obsessing about the holes that you played badly the previous week, think about some different strategies for those same holes. Maybe you can take a different approach or use a different club. Begin to formulate your game plan, addressing all of the issues that gave you problems in your last round. Now forget about your playing strategy for a moment, and think about the fun, relaxing time you'll have with your friends, walking along a beautiful golf course, breathing the fresh air. Calm your mind and being to visualize great shots on all of the holes, especially those that gave you problems before. You'll know exactly how you're going to take the ball from the tee to the green on each one and you'll feel a surge of confidence. In this scenario, you'll arrive at the course feeling calm, peaceful, and ready to take a crack at whatever the course sends your way. In your warm-up, you'll know that it's going to be a great day!

Which scenario would you choose? How you start your game is entirely up to you. When you understand this, there's little excuse for not making the effort to get your game off to a peaceful start. Try it, and you'll surely see that it's worth the effort.

58.

Don't Get
"Over-Golfed"

You probably know several people at your club who are "over-golfed." This doesn't mean that they just play too much, watch golf on TV excessively, or talk about it endlessly. These people join every committee that they can possibly join at the club. They make a big deal out of elections, or walk around the course looking for things to make a fuss about. After a while, they become so involved in the politics of the course that they no longer enjoy going there, but rather feel that they must go there in order to perform the many duties that they've acquired. In the end, they may not play nearly as much golf as they used to play.

Maybe this sounds like you. There's nothing wrong with becoming involved at your club or home course, trying to improve the course or the policies surrounding it. However, it's easy to take it too far. You can become engrossed in so many issues and sit on so many committees that you find yourself rushing around at home to get to the club, and running around the club like crazy to attend every meeting. Suddenly, you discover that you've become so much of an "administrator" that you may not even be playing golf! Now you're more concerned about how the superintendent is cutting the greens, the service in the dining room, or the attitude of the staff.

Who benefits when you become over-golfed? Amazingly, almost no one—least of all you, because you've taken on so much that you're probably not very effective in what you do. The truth is probably that you're no longer having much fun. You may find yourself feeling resentful for all of the time that you spend in meetings, listening to other members' gripes and concerns. Can you even remember why you joined the club in the first place? This is the lot of those who become too involved in organizing and participating.

It's wise to know your limits and stay within them. If you want to become involved in how your club is run, consider your available time before joining committees. Choose one or two that really mean something to you, where you feel that you can truly do some good. Then invest just enough time so that you can be effective and still have plenty of time to play golf—and have a life outside of the club. You'll feel less stressed and enjoy yourself more if you can stop short of becoming over-golfed.

59.

Out of Bounds
Is Part of Golf

Nobody wants to hit a shot out of bounds. It can be difficult to accept that out of bounds is part of golf, and always has been. On the Old Course at St. Andrews in Scotland, out of bounds plays an integral role in the strategy of several holes. But on most courses, it's usually just a boundary marker to tell you that you've hit the ball into someone's backyard. In the last forty years, many narrow, unforgiving golf holes have been constructed where going out of bounds is an ever-present threat. You probably feel like you've played most of them.

Some players are out of bounds nearly as much as they're in bounds, and naturally, they can become quite frustrated. Out of bounds can be especially annoying or uncomfortable if the course is a desert layout with all eighteen holes lined by cactus and snakes or surrounded on all sides by homes.

Unfortunately, the punishment for a lost ball or a shot hit out of bounds is the most severe in all of golf. Take the stroke-and-distance penalty: If you've teed up your ball and sliced it out of bounds, you must verbally declare that you're hitting a "provisional" ball (usually amid deafening silence), tee up another shot, and then tack on a penalty stroke for good measure. If your provisional tee shot is in bounds, then you lie three. If you lose the ball, the situation is even more humbling. You have five minutes maximum to search for it. After that, if the ball can't be found, you must make that painful return to the tee, much to the dismay of the group behind you (unless you had wisely hit a provisional shot to avoid this most awkward of situations). Then you tee off again and hope that you lie three somewhere in play.

Like other aspects of the game that players may feel are unfair, learning to accept out of bounds as part of the game will help to keep you from stressing about it and make it easier for you to work on staying in bounds. You may take some comfort in knowing that going out of bounds is a common error. So don't be discouraged from playing the game of golf as it is meant to be played—with plenty of room for error.

60.

Stop Comparing
Yourself to the Pros

Every golfer wants to play a great game and improve. It's natural to compare your play to that of other golfers as you work to increase your skills. But many players put too much pressure on themselves to perform, believing that they are capable of playing even to the level of the pros. If you must compare your play, compare it to yourself as you watch for incremental improvement in your practice. Comparing yourself to the pros, or even scratch golfing friends, can only end in frustration and disappointment.

There's nothing wrong with having a favorite player that you wish to emulate. You might be an avid fan of that player. But understand that this person has spent many years, countless hours of practice, and much money to become a professional player. Just like models and actors who spend literally hours a day working out in the gym in order to achieve their perfect bodies, professional golfers' lives are their golf games. What the pros achieve isn't usually something that the average person can achieve on weekends, or even several days a week. Many pros start playing golf as children and have access to top training, equipment, and coaches. To have a professional golf career, they give up a lot of what most people would call a "normal" life. More than likely, they also possess a natural talent that—in combination with being in the right place at the right time—leads them to their careers on the tour.

Recreational golfers simply can't live up to expectations of playing like the pros. Having such expectations is just another way of seeking perfectionism, and perfectionism is inconsistent with happiness. It's okay to want to improve and become a better golfer, and you can do that. Work with your trouble areas, learn and take lessons, but most importantly, play golf. The more that you play and enjoy the game, the better that you'll become. You'll find that your own improvements, measured against your own personal, realistic measuring stick, can be their own reward. When you toss aside the pros' measuring stick, you'll be a much happier and more satisfied person.

61.

Go with the Twists, Turns, and Doglegs

Golfers can be pretty amusing. They can complain about boring golf courses, yet complain even more loudly about interesting ones. Why? The most interesting courses are the ones that present challenges! If every hole on every course were straight and wide, you really would get bored. Otherwise, you could slam a golf ball down an airport runway over and over, day after day, and be satisfied.

Some of the most beautiful, challenging, and fun golf courses to play are filled with twists, turns, doglegs, and other great design elements to give you a thrill. A "twist," in this case, means something unusual, out-of-the-ordinary, or just downright surprising. A truly interesting and challenging course provides an occasional twist, and when you come to think of it, that's probably the secret of most of the great holes all over the world. They all have some kind of a twist. The thirteenth at Augusta is the most famous par-5, and for most of its existence, it measured shorter than most long par-4s. Yet it has confused and bewildered more great players than any other hole in golf. The famous Road Hole green at St. Andrews is actually guarded by a road—thus the name—but it's worked that way for nearly 300 years.

The game of golf would be excruciatingly boring without the sometimes irritating twists and turns on courses. Part of the adventure of the game is the mystery of what lies ahead. The key to really enjoying golf is to be open to the unknown challenges and be ready to give them your best.

62.

Accept Praise Graciously

Many people have a difficult time accepting praise with a simple "thank you." Golfers are no different. If someone praises your skill, your mental agility on the course, your driving ability, or perhaps your patience with teaching others, you may brush it off, or even give reasons why you're not really worthy of the praise. Often, it's a fear of seeming conceited that can make you say, "Oh, no, I'm not that good a player."

It may also be a lack of self-confidence. You can have a difficult time seeing in yourself what others see in you, particularly in golf. Think of praise as a gift. If someone gives you a gift just to be nice, you don't give it right back with explanations of why you really shouldn't have it, do you? Then don't do it with the gift of a compliment.

Accepting praise doesn't mean that you're full of yourself. On the other hand, agreeing too strongly with the praise-giver would be conceited. Instead, graciously accept compliments with a simple "thank you," and enjoy the praise. You'll make the other person feel good, too, by accepting the praise in the same spirit in which it was given.

63.

Don't Be a Backseat "Driver"

Can you think of anything more irritating than having someone in the car with you who tells you how to drive, where to turn, what to do, and what not to do? Few people behind the wheel appreciate a backseat driver. With no apologies for the pun, golfers appreciate a backseat "driver" even less. Someone chattering at you about how to make your shot, where to hit it, what to avoid, and other "helpful" hints is without question one of the more irritating things that you can encounter on the golf course. If you've ever had this happen to you, then you know that being a backseat "driver" is a sure way to stymie golf relationships.

You've probably heard it all at one time or another: "You're swinging too fast! Make sure you keep your left arm straight. Your grip just doesn't look right. Your head's coming up too fast! Watch your follow-through! And keep your eye on the ball!" Hopefully, you'll remember how it feels to hear these things if you ever get the urge to offer your partners critiques of their tee shots. While it's almost a natural tendency for most golfers to want to tell someone how to drive, it almost never helps the person. Being distracted by your backseat driving might cause her to hit one bad shot, never hit a decent shot the rest of the day, or ruin her game for weeks! At this point, it can be difficult for even the most congenial personality to take your advice in the well-intentioned manner that it was given, and the person will probably get upset. Some of your more competitive golfer friends may, in fact, think that you're trying to throw them off of their game intentionally. The last thing that you want is such a misunderstanding in your regular group.

If you're compelled to offer golfing advice to your friends and partners, stick to some fairly harmless items, like where to enjoy a great golfing vacation at a nice resort with a challenging course at a reasonable price. Otherwise, avoid the problem of giving advice at all, and leave the driving to the driver.

64.

Embrace Golf's
Endless Variety

To the outsider, golf appears to consist of a bunch of oddly dressed people chasing a little white ball around for hours at a time. Yet the game of golf hooks those who once laughed at it, just as easily as it addicts those who loved it at first sight. Golf is like no other game in the world, thanks to its endless variety.

Golf gives us a multitude of reasons to play. It might be for health or healthy competition or for the thrill of a friendly wager. Some see golf as a great tool to advance their business relationships. Then there are those who are able to put their egos aside (in other words, ignore their scores) and play purely for fun and relaxation.

Golfers can enjoy the variety of playing fields that come in all shapes and sizes and in all different lengths and configurations. In 1903, noted golfer and writer John Low wrote in *Concerning Golf:* "No golfer has ever been forced to say to himself with tears, 'There are no more links to conquer.'" The merits of different courses can be debated almost endlessly, much to the delight of players everywhere. Every golfer is an architect at heart, mentally building his own layout just the way that he thinks a course should play.

There is variety in clubs, swings, and everything in between. Best of all, no other game in the world provides so many ways to achieve personal satisfaction in playing. It's this diversity that makes it nearly impossible to give up on a round of golf. How many times have you sliced wildly into the trees, then salvaged the hole with a heroic recovery shot, then a wedge close to the hole, and a fine putt to save par? At the same time, your partner can be plotting his way efficiently down the fairway, onto the green, and into the hole with two solid putts. It was this potpourri of avenues to the hole that made the game so wildly popular in its earliest days at St. Andrews.

The next time that you tee up or sneak out to the driving range to hit a quick bucket of balls, embrace the endless variety of the game. And don't forget to take a look at the variety of people who play golf. You'll see folks of all shapes and sizes, and an even broader array of personalities—and they all love golf. The universal appeal and the assortment of characters that admire and theorize about the game prove that variety is the very soul of golf.

65.

Vary Your Practices

The game of golf offers you an endless variety of things to enjoy every time that you play, and your practice should reflect the same variety. You may want to work repeatedly on a pesky problem, such as your bunker play, but that shouldn't stop you from practicing your chipping, putting, or iron shots, as well. Keep in mind that practice makes better, so you should cover a number of components of your game when you hit the practice range.

You use all of your clubs when you play, right? So why would you go to the practice range and hit only with your driver? You might become very comfortable with your driver, but should the need arise during a game to use a 2-iron, it might feel unfamiliar to you, and you'll lack confidence with it.

Practicing with all of your clubs at the range will help make you comfortable with every club in the bag, which can go a long way toward improving all areas of your play. Plus, practice won't become boring. Your practice session is also the time to dip into your "old baggage," so to speak, and pull out the mistakes that you've made in previous rounds. Work them out on the practice range by mimicking those same conditions that you encountered on the course. Did your ball lie in the rough or someone's divot? You could also try hitting shots extremely low, practicing your recovery shot from the woods. Create a lot of different situations in practice so that there will be fewer things to surprise you during a game. Then if an unusual situation does present itself, you may have actually played it before, because you created it in your practice session.

Turn your creativity loose when you practice—you can have a lot of fun when you're the one creating your own challenges. If you can get your partners to play along, try practicing together every now and then, and let someone else create a "fine mess" for you to get yourself out of. Think of it as another way for all of you to put the true meaning of the word "play" back into the game. As in life, some of the most interesting and educational experiences can come out of creative golf play. You'll look forward to your practice and get a lot more out of it when you think in terms of variety.

66.

Keep All of
Your Lies True

Have you ever been out playing by yourself for practice or just playing a casual round and found yourself tempted to nudge the ball out of a less than stellar lie? Did you do it, glancing around first to see if anyone was looking? You probably would never consider doing that during a regular round, yet many golfers have a habit of breaking the rules when they're not in competition or if they're playing alone.

The reasoning might sound something like, "Oh, I'm just goofing around," or, "I really don't have time to work out that tough shot today." Golfers who justify rule-breaking in those ways, thinking nothing of nudging their balls, are really just selling themselves short and missing out on some great opportunities. What better time could there be to work out the tough shots than when you're not in competition and just "goofing around"? You aren't playing under pressure, your swing feels okay, and if you're really just having fun, it means that you're probably relaxed and in a pretty good mood. This is when you can really make some progress with tough shots. You can gather experience that will help you visualize your way out of similar situations when they really count.

Then there's the question of ethics. "Play the ball where it lies" is one of the basics of the game. When you keep all of your lies true, especially when you're alone, you're also practicing being ethical by playing fair and following the rules. It becomes a habit, and it's one of the best habits that you can develop. Best of all, you're not letting yourself down, and that's the most important thing in the end.

Playing around the rules isn't really playing golf, whether you're in a tournament, practicing, or just goofing around. When faced with a decision to break the rules or abide by them, it always pays to take the high road, even if you're the only one who knows about it.

67.

Remember
What "Play" Means

Do you get so wrapped up in competition and the need for perfection that you forget to have fun on the golf course? You're far from alone. A lot of golfers start playing the game with the intention of relaxing, having fun, and participating in a sport with their friends. But they end up losing the concept of fun by becoming overly serious about a game that most players are incapable of perfecting. If this sounds like you, it's time to remember what "play" means and take steps to bring it back into your game.

The best way to do this is to watch kids learning the game. They literally play at it, using make-believe and taking a no-score, carefree attitude that most adults could probably stand to try at least now and then. For example, have a "putt-out" with some of your friends. No scores, no round, no wagers, no real practice—just go to the putting green with the firm intention of playing around. Have fun with it, just like the kids do. Make it a completely different experience from how you play your real games. See if you can become so relaxed and unconcerned about how well you're doing that you actually do putt well, or that you learn to shape shots without really trying. Another thing you can do is play a round for a prize that's anything but money. Try dinner, a movie, or a pizza, as long as it's not "serious." Once again, you might find that when there's no real pressure, you can actually have a lot of fun and perhaps begin to see your own play in a different light. The more creative that you can be with your play, the better.

The idea is to try to free your mind from the rigid "adult" restrictions that encumber your game. Adults take their "games" very seriously and often turn into people who aren't welcome in friendly competition. It's always more fun to hang out with those who can let go every now and then, not take life or their golf games so seriously, and just play around when they feel like it.

68.

There's More
Than One Way

If your goal is to improve your game and lower your score, it's helpful to know that there's more than one way to approach your problems. If you're having trouble with bunker shots, the path of your swing, or the shape of your shots, there's rarely a "one-size-fits-all" solution. Your partners, the course pro, and even your teacher may insist that you do things a certain way, but the truth is that their ways won't always work for everyone. If you find yourself frustrated with a method that's not working for you, try another way. You have plenty of options.

If you don't believe it, just look at all the golf books, magazine articles, instruction videos, and teachers available to give you a myriad of ways to fix your swing and short game. Of course, you don't want to confuse yourself or get into information overload. But you may have to try a few things before you find what's right for you.

Some golfers will persist with a certain method, either because it's trendy at the moment, or because someone else had success with it. In a way, it's like trying to force a square peg into a round hole. If it's not right for you, it's just not right for you. You always have to find your own way. Your problems are individual, and your solutions should be, too. Your friend may have been able to improve her swing by working with a certain teacher, for example. You may try a few lessons with this person, but maybe your personalities don't click as well, and you find that this teacher can't tell where you're not quite getting it. If you're uncomfortable working with this teacher, it's not going to get you anywhere. Another friend may turn to new equipment as a way to become better at iron play. But often, it's not really the equipment that makes the difference—rather, a shift in your frame of mind is what's really responsible. Thus making an expensive equipment purchase might not do you a bit of good, even if your friend found it helpful.

Check out all of your options, but don't stress out over the many choices available to you. Take your time, try out a couple different teachers, or read a few books. The stress of continuing to try something that's not working can be worse than feeling stuck with your problem. Eventually, you'll find what's right for you, and as you begin to improve, you'll be much happier that you took the time to find your own way.

69.

Play One
Stroke at a Time

Every golfer has at least one hole on a favorite course that's a personal "bugaboo." Perhaps it's the hole that poses the biggest personal challenge, or it's the one where you seem unable to make par, no matter how well you're playing. Maybe you even have a superstition about playing the hole and feel that you just can't get a lucky break. Whatever the case, you've managed to turn it into something that causes you distress out of proportion to its importance. The best way to approach such a hole is to make the conscious decision to play it one stroke at a time.

If you think about it, you're probably playing the hole in its entirety each time you reach it. Because it's a challenge, you might remember in vivid detail every time that you bogeyed it (or worse), every shot that landed in the water or in the bunker, and every game in which it stands out as the worst hole of all eighteen. This kind of negative thinking can snowball and spiral into tension and anxiety.

On the hole that gives you fits, negative thinking can take you to the putt before you've even teed off! At that point, you're so concerned about the last stroke that you aren't giving full attention to your first stroke. That's often how the entire hole winds up being a disaster.

To really concentrate on your game and play the hole one stroke at a time, you need to head off this kind of thinking before it has a chance to build momentum. You might notice it as you approach the hole, when you find yourself thinking back to the last time that you played it. Try to consciously nip the process in the bud by saying to yourself, "That was then—this is now. It's a new day, and I'm starting from stroke one." Then your focus isn't on how overwhelmed you feel facing your most challenging hole, but on how you'll tackle it today by playing it one stroke at a time.

The next time that you feel your heart rate pick up as you approach the hole, try this strategy to calm yourself. Get ready to attack it stroke by stroke. You'll be surprised at how effective it can be.

70.

Separate Golf
from Everything Else

Golfers love the game. Some worship the game. When they're not playing golf, they're watching it on TV, reading about it, or talking about it. They may truly enjoy living life this way, but they often do so at the expense of their relationships with non-golfer family and friends. If you love the game, it is helpful to be aware that sometimes you have to separate golf from other areas of your life.

This means consciously observing your behavior to avoid irritating non-golfers, and making sure that golf doesn't take up every moment of your life. Look for the clues. If the faces of your family members fall when you announce that you're going out to play a round, it could mean that you're playing so much that they never have time with you. When in conversation with non-golfers, see if you can possibly not discuss yesterday's birdie on the eighteenth hole or complain about last week's tragic triple-bogey that cost you the club championship. People get bored when all you do is talk about yourself or your interests and don't show any enthusiasm for them and theirs. If your TV is always tuned to a golf game or clinic, try turning the TV off and doing something else for a change. Similarly, when you're visiting someone, don't immediately turn their TV on to the tour.

It's okay to love the game of golf and want to immerse yourself in it, but not at the expense of your family life and other relationships. A healthy balance between golf and the rest of your life is what will keep the stress down and make you—and everyone around you— much happier. Golf isn't everything. Be sure to enjoy other activities and people in your life, too.

71.

Give Your
Partners a Break

If you have a steady group of people that you golf with regularly, and especially if you've been together for a long time, you can probably liken your interaction to the dynamic of a family. You're privy to their life's problems and worries. You are often forced to deal with their annoying habits. When they're playing well and you're game isn't quite in top form, you may have to listen to some bragging. You may also listen to bragging about their children or grandchildren. Basically, you go through all the good and bad things that people who are close to each other share.

Just remember that your partners have to deal with you, too! Just as you handle their quirks and the problems that they may discuss with you, they have to handle yours, as well. From their perspective, you may be even more difficult to deal with than they are. Take a moment, and think about some of the things about your partners that can annoy you from time to time.

Now take a step back, and try to look at yourself from their point of view. Do you see some of the same types of behavior? If you're playing a terrific game and they're not, are you making light of their plight? Do you find their pre-shot routines or the ways they mark their balls on the greens annoying? By putting yourself in their shoes, you can see that the little annoyances you face from them are no different from the little irritations that they put up with from you. Your group would do well to understand that all people see things from their own perspectives. It can serve you well to be sympathetic to another's point of view.

A good way to do that is to focus not on what your partners do wrong, but on what they do right. You'll come to realize that most of the time, you all get along well and have great fun playing golf together. Now, when the little irritations occur, it's easier to avoid blowing them out of proportion. You may not be able to change how others behave, but you can certainly change your own reactions to them. When you give your partners a break, they'll appreciate it and will likely return the favor. Then you'll all bring out the best in each other and make the rounds of golf that you share something truly enjoyable that you can all look forward to.

72.

Develop a
Reset Button

You may not know it, but you've probably developed stress patterns on the golf course that you tend to repeat over and over. Think about the times that you're most agitated, and try to understand the thoughts and feelings that precede the stress. Those are your warning signals. You can learn to listen to these signals and stop frustration in its tracks by pushing your own "reset button." You'll regain your perspective and break a painful cycle.

Here's how to do this: You must first be able to recognize the warning signals that you're becoming overly stressed. Maybe your heart rate picks up or your hands get sweaty. Maybe you get a feeling of being under pressure, or your mind starts to wander. Whatever the signs, as soon as you notice them, mentally push your reset button by saying to yourself, "Okay, it's time to reset," or, "Here I go again." Now, you can take a moment to start over, regroup, or reset, by slowing down and taking a deep breath. Count to ten. You might even think of the word "relax" repeatedly as you breathe. Once you settle down, you can get back to your game feeling calm, which will allow you to play better.

The great thing about this strategy is that you can carry it over into your everyday life. Look for your stress signals at home and at work, and learn to use your reset button in those circumstances. You may find that you can get an upper hand on the stresses in your life away from the golf course, as well.

73.

Learn to
Stay Centered

When you think of the word "centered," it implies being in the middle, or in balance. If you're centered, you have balance in life, allowing you to stay on an even keel both physically and mentally. You're able to handle life's emergencies in a calm, collected manner, and keep from being thrown off by unexpected events and circumstances. As a golfer, these qualities can be beneficial to your game. The concept of balance is good for you to carry over from life on to the golf course.

Staying centered emotionally keeps you calm and able to concentrate on your game plan. Your mind is focused, or centered, on your shot. Physically, your swing is centered and balanced when you keep your head still and over the center of the ball and your body aligned properly. There's a sense of comfort and calm when you can keep your head still and not sway too far backward or forward. When you combine physical and mental balance, you'll feel better prepared to handle the unpredictable things that occur during the course of play.

Being centered in golf and in life all comes down to one thing: learning to keep your attention in the present moment. On the golf course, staying in the present can keep you from feeling stress and let you focus on the shot at hand. If you give too much attention to your thoughts and find yourself worrying about what lies ahead or obsessing about a mistake that you just made, you'll probably see that you're having a more difficult time with your game. Your mind wanders, and your body becomes tense and rigid. When you can bring yourself back to center, you'll achieve a sense of mental balance that automatically relaxes your body. You'll experience good and bad shots with the same level of acceptance and spirit of play.

The concept of staying centered is a good one as applied to golf. It has a Zen feel to it, as well as practical use in both the mental and physical games. Keep all your attention centered in the moment by not worrying about the next hole or being upset about the last one, and you'll be better able to make your current shot the best one that you can hit.

74.

Stop Magnifying
Your Flaws

Peole have a need to be critical. They place small imperfections under a magnifying glass and enlarge them. Golfers do this by being highly judgmental of how others play, as well as criticizing their own play. At the clubhouse after a round, you can revel in telling a crowd how one of your partners blew it on the third hole and couldn't seem to recover. You discuss another golfer's mistakes as if you don't make any yourself. Sometimes, it seems you never give a word of praise for others. It can make people wonder where the concept of "camaraderie" has gone in the game of golf. For some golfers, magnifying the flaws of others can actually be a form of entertainment, and we can always find plenty of others willing to play along.

Even worse, you can be the hardest on yourself. While you may have posted a round a shot or two below your handicap, you instead discuss endless details of how you blew a chance to post your best score ever. The frustration and anger that you can feel at yourself doesn't always go away easily, because you've made a mental habit out of magnifying your flaws. When you're done with one flaw, you look for another. It's one thing to look at the flaws in your play with an eye toward working on problems in your practice sessions. It's another thing if you beat yourself up about every minor problem. Reminding yourself of your mistakes over and over can actually keep you from correcting them when you practice, because your negative thinking is in control.

It's important to be aware of your critical thinking and break the habit of holding a magnifying glass too close. Learning to be less judgmental of yourself and others can take a lot of stress and pressure off of you. When you're no longer obsessed with finding flaws and making them bigger than they are, you'll have more time to relax and enjoy golf, as well as the company of your friends. This is a good strategy to practice in every aspect of your life, not just on the golf course. Magnifying flaws is a negative mental habit that you can break. Learn to give credit to yourself and others for the positives, too.

75.

Take the Game
as It Comes

One of the great things about golf is that each game is different. It doesn't matter if you're playing on the same course every day or with the same partners, the game always finds a way to present you with wind coming from a different direction, faster greens, or simply days when your touch feels hot. Because of this, golfers who approach the game with expectations of how it will play out are often disappointed, because the game rarely turns out as they expect it to turn out. It is exactly what it is—nothing more, nothing less.

Okay, sometimes the game does turn out to be what you expect, as when you play to your handicap but still struggle with the same shots. You haven't been able to work it out yet and you're practicing. But what tends to cause stress and anxiety is when you expect things to go well and they don't. Or they do go well, but you want them to be better. No matter what you do, it seems that you can't enjoy the game because you always wish that it had turned out differently.

After a round, do you talk about the good things that happened, or do you tend to focus on what went wrong? Do you feel good for having played that day, or are you upset and tense because your play wasn't up to your expectations? For many golfers, their enjoyment of golf can often be measured by how much they accept what happens when they play versus how upset they become if things don't go as expected. If this sounds like you, it may be time to lower your expectations and work toward becoming more accepting of what is.

The fact is that many things will occur on the golf course that you can't predict or change, and that are completely beyond your control. When those things occur, isn't it better to take them in stride and make the best of them, rather than struggle against them? Learning to practice peaceful acceptance on the golf course can help you become less stressed, and you'll probably play better because of it.

76.

Think About Plays
That You Made Correctly

Take a moment right now to consider how often you think about and keep track of the mistakes that you make during a golf game or when you're practicing. You may say to yourself, "I can't believe I sliced it out of bounds (or missed another short putt, or hit five inches behind the ball again)." Now, can you think of an equal number of things that you've given yourself credit for? The vast majority of golfers spend more time focusing on what's wrong than on what's right. There's a price to be paid for this kind of thinking, and becoming stressed out, self-defeating, and uptight are the results.

Nobody's perfect—that's a fact. You have to give yourself a break and accept that there's no way you'll hit every shot perfectly or score your lowest in every game that you play. The truth is that if everything about your golf game were perfect, you'd probably be bored to tears and give up the sport! But focusing all of your attention on your inability to correct common faults can only discourage you.

Shifting your focus to what you're doing right, however, lets you deal with your problems simply because you feel better about yourself. You become more patient with your mistakes and can practice more effectively. Negative thinking can make you feel like practice is punishment for being a bad player, but positive focus lets you see it as working toward improvement.

If golfers could become half as good at positive self-talk as they are at negative self-talk, play would probably improve greatly on golf courses worldwide! Remember that just as you learn from mistakes, you can learn from the things that you do right, and you'll be more likely to repeat them. As in all of life, do the best that you can on the course, and let the mistakes go. Then you'll really start having fun with golf, and that's what you truly wanted when you took up the game in the first place.

77.

Be an Example
of Good Sportsmanship

Bad sportsmanship is more prevalent than ever in both amateur and professional arenas. You can barely watch a football, basketball, or baseball game—even a golf match—without seeing at least one example of really poor sportsmanship. It's always disturbing, but even more so when young people are watching it happen.

In golf, following the rules of etiquette and keeping emotions under control are very important to the game. No one likes to play with someone who gets frustrated and angry, throws clubs, argues, or cheats. Nor do players want to be around someone who is constantly explaining away bad shots. People love being around a good sport—someone who follows the rules, plays the game calmly and with integrity, accepts bad breaks and defeats graciously, and always plays golf for fun and enjoyment, if not a little healthy competition. The emphasis here needs to be on the word "healthy," since some competitors can truly make a round of golf ugly by being too competitive. There's rarely a good, positive end to such unhealthy, aggressive games.

All golfers should strive to be examples of calm play and good sportsmanship for others. You can do that by being consistent in behavior, keeping emotions in check, and always opting for the honorable solution when questions of rules arise. When you maintain this attitude and present yourself as practicing good sportsmanship, it can only help to bring out the best in those around you, as well. You open the door for others to follow your example and create an environment where it's okay to go with the flow.

The first step is to acknowledge integrity and good sportsmanship as goals and priorities in your game. In fact, make them your top priorities, and you'll find that others will respect you for it. It's okay to be competitive—that's also a big part of what golf is all about. But it's important to keep honor, integrity, and sportsmanship paramount in golf. How you behave is always within your control. You can choose to practice good sportsmanship for yourself and for the good of the game.

78.

Remember That
This Game, Too, Shall End

There's an old saying that every golfer would do well to remember: "This, too, shall pass." This bit of wisdom sounds simple, and it is. But it can help you overcome those annoyances, irritations, and frustrations you face on the golf course, particularly on those days when it seems that nothing can go right.

Think of it this way: The round starts and it ends. You play badly, and then you play well. You could top one shot ten yards off the tee, but then hit a 240-yard drive on the next hole. Or you may miss a three-footer on one green, and then drain a sixty-footer two holes later. That's how it goes each and every time that you're on the golf course, the practice range, or the putting green. It's a cycle of change, like the seasons, and appreciating this fact can help you keep things in perspective—especially on those really bad days. When you approach a bad game knowing that it will end and another cycle will surely begin, you won't feel quite as bad.

Sometimes, you can feel as if you're caught in a streak of bad luck, and you might think to yourself, "I'll never be able to make another putt ever again!" That one thought alone can overwhelm you, thus affecting the rest of your game and really dragging out your problems. But remembering that it's just a phase in your game and it will pass will lighten the load on your mind. You can take the bad strikes or struggles with the putter in stride and move on.

It's the same way in life. Seasons come and seasons go; joy, sorrow, hardships, accomplishments, fun, pain—you've been through them all. Looking back, you can see how things always change. The trick is to remember this dynamic while you're going through something difficult. Another old saying brings home the point, as well: "Nothing lasts forever." That goes for bad days on the golf course, too. There's always another day, so remember that a bad game—and bad hits, bad lies, bad weather, and bad luck—will end.

79.

Avoid the 80–20 Trap

This is a habit that people fall into in all areas of their lives, but when golfers fall into the 80–20 trap, it can be worse than landing in a bunker! People have a tendency to focus on the negative things in life and brush aside the positive things, even when their lives contain mostly good. On the golf course, the 80–20 trap occurs when golfers place all of their attention on the worst twenty percent of a course or hole (bunkers, roughs, and hazards) instead of the other eighty percent (fairways and greens). This can cause a lot of anxiety as you see and anticipate every little problem and hassle, rather than going with the flow and playing the course for what it is.

By seeing only the roughs and hazards, you place a lot of stress on yourself, and the tension can ruin your game. Try this instead: Stand and look at a hole before you, and make a determination in your mind of how much of the hole is hazard and how much of it is a really great place that you can hit the ball to. The majority of the time, you'll see that the hole is probably eighty percent fairway and putting surface, and about twenty percent rough, sand, and possibly water. So the hole just isn't as bad as you might first think. There's plenty of room to hit and quietly work your way to the hole while avoiding the hazards.

The idea here is to become aware of any tendency that you might have to get yourself tense and worked up because you see the tough spots on the hole more clearly than you can see your way to the pin. If you can shift your focus to the positive eighty percent of the hole, you may find that you're able to visualize a creative game plan. You'll feel more relaxed and able to actually put that plan into action, and you'll be more able to make those great shots in your mind a reality. Seeing that there are far more positive things about a hole can give you a more positive outlook in general, and that will lift your spirits and make you feel better.

That's not to say that you should pretend that the twenty percent of roughs and hazards aren't there. Rather keep them in perspective, and instead of seeing obstacles that can't be surmounted, you'll realize that they're obstacles that can be negotiated in plenty of ways. See if you can practice avoiding the 80–20 trap and really experience and enjoy the other part of the golf course. You'll find that you enjoy your round much more, and you may even improve your score when you can see, plan, and play to the best eighty percent.

80.

Become a Little
Less Stubborn

One of the biggest contributors to slow play is a stubborn player. Many problems can occur on the course when players argue stubbornly about who's right and who's wrong about a rule, a lie, or most anything else.

Stubbornness is easy to detect in others but often very hard to see in ourselves. You've probably run into stubborn kids who announced, "I am not stubborn!" Golfers can be much the same way. When you refuse to play by the rules or take advice about your game the right way, you'll see this quality rear its ugly head.

If you're stubborn, you're usually tense because you're walking around with a rigid mindset. You don't want to listen to others' opinions or try to see others' points of view. You're often on the defensive. You dig your heels in and won't budge. Thus when your group is trying to figure out whose turn it is to play or what the proper ruling is for a tricky situation, you can actually slow the game down with your stubborn attitude. Even worse, when you're stubborn, you have a tendency to insist that you are always right. In order to do that, you go out of your way to find mistakes and point out where you perceive others to be wrong. Doing this creates frustration and irritation, and alienates you from everyone that you come into contact with.

There's a simple solution to the problem of being stubborn: Learn to say "You're right." The hard part is really meaning it! Stubborn people, of course, will stubbornly refuse, and say, "Why should I say that she's right if she's not right?" The answer is because learning to say "You're right" and meaning it is a humbling thing, and it goes to the core of easing stubborn attitudes. Being stubborn is stressful, and becoming less stubborn makes you feel free. When you're not stressed out, you play better golf. If you can relax your attitude, you'll relax your body and mind, and that's one of the best things you can do for your game, and for your relationships with others.

Saying "You're right" is certainly easier said than done. It takes practice to become less stubborn, but you have to start somewhere. So the next time you face the question of who is farther away from the hole or who is right about a bizarre ruling, try to keep an open mind about the arguments and ease up. Become a little less stubborn, and move the game along. You'll feel better, too, when you learn that you don't always have to be right.

81.

Get Yourself—and Your
Game—in Balance

We've all had times when things in our lives seem to careen out of control. You feel like your work has become too much, the kids are acting too rambunctious, there are too many bills, and you don't have enough time for yourself. What you once looked forward to as social situations, you now call "social obligations." You might even find yourself saying something like, "I *have* to play golf tomorrow," and if that's the case, something's wrong. With that attitude, your game is probably all over the place when you do get a chance to play. You can't seem to work out your problems, and your score creeps upward instead of down. What's wrong with this picture?

It could be that you simply have too much on your plate, to the point where fun isn't fun anymore. It may be time to get your life in balance by making some changes in your priorities. Even little changes can help you to see things more clearly, take life's hectic pace more calmly, and handle many things at once more effectively.

The trick is to prioritize your obligations and responsibilities to see what's really important and what isn't.

Take work, for example. If you're always at the office and can't seem to break away, you might consider delegating some of your responsibilities. This can free up your time again so you can be with your family and friends, get things done at home, and enjoy playing golf once again. You might cut back on social obligations by learning to say no to invitations once in a while without feeling guilty about it. That "relaxing" weekend at your brother's might not relax you nearly as much as one good day on the golf course, especially if you know up front that visiting your relatives won't be relaxing at all.

When prioritizing and trying to bring some balance back into your life, realize that you can't do everything, and you certainly don't have to "do it all." There's a bit of perfectionism in everyone that can make you think that you have to take on everything and do it all well. The fact is that you'll be less stressed and enjoy all of your activities more, from work to play, if you learn to slow down life's pace and keep it all in balance. So ease up on your schedule, and as someone who loves golf, make a regular, relaxing game a top priority in your life. Instead of "I *have* to play golf," you'll hear yourself saying, "I *want* to play golf."

82.

Your Emotions Affect Your Play

Recognizing how your emotions affect your play is important, because emotions can make or break your golf game. When you lose control of your emotions, you've lost control of your game.

Negative emotions running amok can destroy your mental game. It's impossible to focus on each shot when your mind is filled with negative thoughts and feelings, or you're so stressed that your hands are shaking. Not only that, but negative feelings can keep you from correcting any mistakes that you're making by actually reinforcing those mistakes! When you think, "I'm playing lousy today," you are—and you will. On the other hand, controlled and positive emotions can work to your advantage and have the opposite effect. Thinking positive thoughts helps you overcome mistakes and visualize great shots.

How do you get a handle on your emotions in order to play your best? Understand that your feelings and emotions are directly tied to your thinking. It's easy to prove—just try being angry without first thinking about something that makes you angry! You can't do it. It's the same way with other feelings. If you're thinking about something frustrating, you feel frustrated. If you have stressful thoughts, you become stressed out. Think of these situations as "thought attacks."

During your game, a thought attack might show itself like this: You've just topped your first tee shot, and you think to yourself, "I always hit a bad tee shot on the first hole." This leads to other thoughts, like, "I can't get control of it," or, "This is exactly how I mess up my round every time!" Soon, you're so upset and frustrated that you'll almost certainly ruin your game. You are the victim of a thought attack—a progression of thoughts that keep you focused on the negative aspect of a situation and snowball out of your control. You must nip this kind of thinking in the bud! Instead of letting your negative thoughts grow, learn to catch yourself in the act and think instead, "Whoops! There I go again!" or some other personal key phrase that lets you know that you're about to get crazy in your thinking. You can get out of your head and into the present moment—and back to your game.

Remember, your thoughts are just thoughts, and they can't hurt you or your game without your consent. Whenever you recognize that you have control over your behavior, you can choose to dismiss a negative thought and avoid the emotions that come with it. This strategy takes practice, but knowing that you can improve your mental game this way will make it well worth the effort.

83.

Play to Your Strengths,
Accept Your Weaknesses

Can you remember a time in your life when you tried hard to do something that you didn't particularly have a talent for? Perhaps you worked hard at your task and succeeded. Or perhaps you felt that all your hard work wasn't getting you anywhere and you moved on to other horizons. Either way, you learned something along the way. The fact is that everyone has strengths in certain areas and weaknesses in others, and that includes your golf game. You can't do everything well. Learning to recognize your own strengths and weaknesses in your golf game can help you use them strategically when you play.

As you create your game plan so that you can play each hole to the best of your ability, remind yourself of what you are good at and really use those strengths. For example, if you are a good putter from a long way out, but not so hot on the short putts, just remind yourself that you probably aren't three-putting any more than the next player because you're so adept with the long putts. You can also make your practice sessions and lessons more productive when you can honestly admit where you need work. Just be sure to look for the small improvements, and don't expect huge leaps of improvement overnight.

This strategy is important to remember when dealing with others, as well. When partners know and are patient with each other's strengths and weaknesses, they can create a stronger team and work with one another, rather than against one another. Most importantly, you won't have unrealistic expectations of yourself or of others. You'll all be able to cut yourself some slack in those areas where you're not as skilled. Then you'll spend less time grappling with perfectionism, and more time enjoying your golf game and the company of your friends.

84.

Learn to Chill Out

Have you ever heard someone tell a stressed-out golfer to "chill out"? When stress and emotions get out of hand during a round or you feel overwhelmed by the challenges of your game, literally chilling out—cooling down those hot emotions and feelings—is exactly what's needed. It can improve your game and help keep your relationships intact.

Chilling out uses a simple meditation technique that takes the example of quieting your mind between shots a few steps further. It involves deep breathing, counting, and feeling a cool breeze soothe and calm you. It's pretty simple. When you feel yourself getting hot under the collar either on the course or the practice range, take a long, deep breath, close your eyes if possible, and say the word "one" to yourself. Say it softly, or speak it in your mind. Also, visualize the word "one" or the numeral "1" in your mind. Then let out your breath and relax your muscles. As you move on to the number two, imagine a nice, cool breeze blowing across your arms, face, and neck.

Think of a time when you felt greatly relaxed and a cool breeze blowing over your body was part of the experience. Better yet, remember a time when you were on top of your game and you could feel a wonderful breeze. Put yourself into that time and place, feeling the breeze calming and soothing your mind, frazzled nerves, and inflamed emotions—and remember how terrific your game was that day. Feel that breeze again as you continue counting to ten.

If you're really tense, you may need to count further than ten. But this process can really bring down your stress level and imbue your body with an overall calm. When you're finished, you should be able to examine your frustration with a different perspective and continue your game in a much better frame of mind. Players who practice this form of meditation say that they can eventually call up the cool breeze on a moment's notice and chill out under most any circumstance. Yes, it all sounds a bit Zen, and it is! But with so much emphasis being placed on the mental game and the proper state of mind for playing golf, you shouldn't feel funny practicing the "chill-out" technique. In fact, when other players see your results, they may ask you for some tips on cooling down themselves.

85.
Don't Get
"Lessoned Out"

Golf lessons are good for all players, but it is possible to overdo it. There is such a thing as having too much information. When you're thinking about so many different elements of the game, it's no wonder that you still don't have a swing!

Players who get "lessoned out" run the risk of becoming obsessed with swing analysis. The affliction is characterized by an incessant need to analyze your swing on video, to read every book and magazine article that comes along, and sometimes to get up and watch the Golf Channel in the middle of the night. Yet all that information may not help you improve one bit. For one thing, you'll have too much going on in your head to make any sense of it. But more importantly, none of the information is focused specifically on your individual swing.

What can you do? By all means, take lessons—in moderation—because that's the only real way to work with your specific swing problems. You wouldn't watch a TV show or read an article to self-diagnose a disease, would you? So why try to improve your swing with the help of an unseen golf writer or a video commentator who can't see you? Most players do well if they have a regular teacher and stick with that person. The trick to getting the most out of your lessons is to keep your teacher focused on leaving you with only one or two thoughts. If he throws tip after tip at you, it can leave you in shambles. You'll walk away from your lesson thinking that there is too much work to be done to ever improve. When you work on one or two things at a time, you'll see the light at the end of the tunnel.

It's tempting to learn as much as you possibly can about the game, but understand that you really can make matters worse if you get "lessoned out." That's a lesson that you don't need to learn the hard way.

86.

Pros Miss
Three-Foot Putts, Too

Everyone dreads short putts, especially on ultra-fast greens where putting is particularly treacherous. They're supposed to be easy, after all, when it's a mere three feet to the hole, and you can feel pretty bad when you miss such an "easy" putt. But instead of becoming frustrated when you do, remember that even the most seasoned pros miss them, too.

Yes, the three-footers and other short putts are everyone's problem. Chi Chi Rodriguez once said, "I don't fear death...but I sure do hate those three-footers for par." Why? The pressure is on. You're three feet—or less—away from par, or perhaps a birdie. The hole starts to look awfully small, while the putter feels awkward in your hands, and you think about how easy it should be to make such a short putt. No wonder your palms are sweaty and your hands are shaking! If you examine why you miss the short putts, you may find that the way you're thinking under pressure saps your confidence.

Confidence is an important quality when it comes to sinking putts, and the way to get more confident in your putting is to practice, practice, practice. Remember, too, how your thinking affects your emotions. If you beat yourself up every time that you miss a putt, long or short, your negative thoughts will translate into negative emotions that set a bad tone for the rest of your game. Instead, put a positive spin on it by learning from the mistake and working on why you missed the putt.

You also must realize that the rest of the human race—including pros—all feel, or have felt, the same fears and lack of confidence when faced with putts of all lengths. When you miss any putt, including the dreaded three-footer, you can either see yourself as a victim of circumstance, or you can learn from the experience and accept it as part of the game. Golf is full of challenges, obstacles, setbacks, difficulties, and problems for all players, pro and weekender alike. Approach the obstacles with relish, and see each game—and each putt—as a fresh, new challenge. Spend time on the practice green and make those putts, because that's how you get confidence in your putting ability. When it comes to the short putts, you can put yourself in a class with the pros!

87.

Remember
the Golden Rule

Everyone knows that the Golden Rule is to treat others the way that you would like to be treated. In golf, this principle is really one of the basics of etiquette. There are so many ways that golfers can irritate, bother, offend, and otherwise upset each other. You know what irritates you most—can you spot those behaviors in yourself and nip them in the bud? Remember to give other players a break by practicing the Golden Rule of Golf: Treat other players the way that you would like to be treated. And don't forget some of the rule's important corollaries.

- Stay out of another player's line. It's not a rule of the game, but when you're on the green, it's a common courtesy not to walk on the probable line that someone's going to putt over. Notice how the pros will take a wide arc—sometimes an exaggerated arc—to avoid stepping in someone's line, even a potential line. This is worth your close attention.

- Keep your mouth shut after a partner's bad hole. Of course, this is when it's the most tempting to offer some advice, but it's guaranteed to be the worst time, too, so leave it alone and keep playing.

- Keep your mouth shut when your partner's having a great round. This is one of those unspoken rules of golf. It's similar to baseball, when a pitcher is throwing a no-hitter. No one talks to him between innings. It's a superstition, to be sure, but consider that your partner might be in the zone and not want to leave it. So please do not disturb.

- Don't criticize a friend's home course. You don't want anyone knocking your home course, do you? Even if someone plays on the worst course ever, don't explain how you would redesign it. One of the great things about golf is the variety of courses on which it is played.

There's little argument that these simple rules are golden. Everyone who plays golf can appreciate them in practice.

88.

Don't Try to
Explain a Bad Score

Golfers have a way of trying to explain bad scores. "I really didn't feel very well today, so it threw me off on the seventh, and it was downhill from there." Okay, that may be true. But if the next day, the same player says, "Well, we'll see if my back can hold up today," and the game after that says, "I wonder if the swing will ever work," you'll begin to wonder if this golfer ever has fun. It's quite possible for a golfer to have a bad score simply because she had a bad score. It's also possible to have a bad score and not make excuses for it.

It's not just golfers. People, in general, seem to have a need to find excuses for problems or when things go wrong. Life (or golf) doesn't just simply happen in their world. There always has to be a reason for everything. Suppose your neighbor came to your home every day and explained in great detail why her fence was broken. You'd eventually get fed up with the excuses, and as soon as you saw her coming, you'd probably run and hide.

It's no different in your foursome. If you or one of the other players always ends the round with a lengthy analysis of why your score was bad—even if it really wasn't that bad—it can serve to alienate the other players at some point. What you really need to do is discover why you must have an excuse in the first place. If you can stop yourself from needing an excuse for everything that happens, you'll begin to accept things as they arise, and that's a less stressful, more peaceful way to approach both life and your favorite game.

The truth is that golfers don't want to hear your excuses, and really don't care why you've scored badly. In some cases, your more competitive partners may even wish that you'd scored higher. So it's best to just remain silent. Accept your bad scores, and learn from them. Carry those reasons over to your practice sessions to help your focus on your problem areas, but otherwise, keep them to yourself.

89.

Take Lessons
from the Pros

There's a lot to be said about learning to play golf just by doing, particularly for young people who haven't been overly schooled and who can emulate good players without trying very hard. But most golfers get to a point where they need a little help to fix stubborn problems and learn new ways of doing things. That's the time to sign up for some lessons from your local golf pro.

Actually, the pro doesn't really have to be local. You could take a trip and enjoy a weekend of golf at another club, perhaps enrolling in a golf school or seeking out a noted golf resort instructor. But it does help to get to know your local pros and take some lessons on your own turf. This way, you can develop a relationship with a teacher who can get to know your weak spots. You, in turn, can find a teacher who matches your style and personality, someone you can be comfortable with and really enjoy learning from. As you work on your short game or improve your swing mechanics, your teacher can monitor your progress and make sure that you are headed in the right direction.

You might get frustrated trying to correct your own problems with the help of magazine articles and videotapes. Subscribing to all the golf magazines, surfing Internet golf sites, and spending time watching videos or "how-to" TV shows can be interesting and enjoyable, but you'll probably be bombarded with free advice that isn't personalized to your specific problems.

If the cost of lessons makes you think twice, you might try thinking again. Once you add up what you spend on videos, magazines, and extra time on the range, you might find that a few lessons cost the same or less. And even if they set you back a bit more, it may be worth it if you can finally eliminate problematic swing tendencies. You'll feel less frustrated, play better, and enjoy the game much more. That alone may be worth the cost.

90.

Don't Let Your Warm-Up
Dictate Your Game

Have you ever let a bad warm-up session ruin your game? It's not hard to do if you base your game plan on what happens in your warm-up. The problem is that the conditions on the practice range can be vastly different from what you encounter on the course. This is why your game plan should always be based on how your game fits the course that you're playing, not how well or badly you did in your warm-up session. The fact is that you can have a bad warm-up session and end up playing a terrific game, or have a great warm-up and play a miserable round.

Remember the purpose of your warm-up routine. It's to "warm up" your body, loosen those muscles, shake out the cobwebs, and get yourself relaxed but still focused. You want to find your tempo and get a feel for your swing so that you can be as comfortable as possible when you get to the first tee. Your warm-up should be a positive experience that readies you to take on the challenges of the game ahead of you.

What you shouldn't expect from your warm-up is a preview of the course that you'll play. Don't ever try to judge your distances by how the ball flies on the range. Yardage targets are usually not accurate, and range balls are nothing like real balls. The flight pattern of your shots is distorted by this fact alone. If you create your game plan based on your warm-up, you'll probably set yourself up for disappointment. It's true that a good warm-up can put you in great spirits, and that can certainly have a positive effect on your game. But letting a poor warm-up put you in a bad mood can definitely have the opposite effect.

If you've had a bad warm-up, remember that it doesn't have to translate to a bad round if you accept the session for what it was and leave it behind. Some of the best players have reported that they had terrible warm-up sessions before going out and firing their best scores ever, while others have reported the opposite: They left all of their great ball-striking on the range. Create your game plan the way that it should be done, and then stick to it, no matter what happens on the practice range.

91.

Play the
Mental Game

Everyone talks about playing the "mental game" of golf, but exactly what does that mean? It means using your head to play golf and learning to deal with your problems and fears in a rational, relaxed manner.

For example, your mind can be full of chatter on the golf course, and unfortunately, it's usually negative chatter. You berate yourself for a mistake and end up so tense that you can't concentrate on your next shot. Here is where you see that your mind can be your enemy—or your ally. If you hear constant noise in your head scolding you for a bad swing, the effect on your next move isn't likely to be positive. Set the mental noise aside, and quiet your mind instead. File away any problems that you'd like to work on in practice, but get past them in the game, and put your focus onto your next shot.

A crucial element of your mental game is what you tell yourself you need to accomplish versus what you are able to do. Too many golfers set goals for themselves that they know they really can't reach. That's a sure way to defeat yourself at the outset. While you may want to break 80 for the first time, try for 85 instead. You'll probably reach it a lot sooner, and when you do, your confidence will get a terrific boost. Examine the goals that you've set, and make sure that you're not putting too much pressure on yourself. Don't feel guilty for making changes to your goals—or even your game plan. Being able to adapt and make changes is an important part of the mental game. Most golf courses are designed to challenge you. Don't let them throw you. Remember that things aren't always going to go as expected. You'll remain open to making changes in your game plan and be able to go with the flow.

With practice, you can learn to get past the negative thinking that can accompany you on the golf course. When you're calm about the game and your place in it, playing the mental game can turn the tide in your favor.

92.

Become a
Less Aggressive Putter

Many golfers feel that they are most uptight when they're driving, and thus have a tendency to walk up to the tee and whack the ball as hard as they can. Others believe they are at their most aggressive on the green, putting a lot of power into their putts and shooting past the hole more often than not. The green is where a little finesse would probably do some good. It can be helpful to become a less aggressive putter.

Some players have a tendency to try to ram the ball into the hole—an approach that leads to anger and frustration if you end up missing the putt. If you're an aggressive putter, you might want to try something different. There are several schools of thought about putting, of course, but one of the simplest and least stressful philosophies involves trying to tap the ball at just the right speed for it to roll gently to the cup and "die," or just fall right in. This is how Ben Crenshaw does it, and he's widely considered the best putter in golf, perhaps of all time. A more aggressive approach than this can often send your ball past the cup, leaving you with stressful short putts—and more work. Using Crenshaw's concept, you'll develop touch and feel, have an easier time visualizing your line and speed, and sink more putts. The best part about less aggressive putting is that if you do miss the putt, you'll probably end up with a "tap-in."

As with driving, you don't have to smash or overpower the ball when you putt. In fact, taking a more relaxed, gentle approach to putting is a great way to finish the hole. It can help put you in a more peaceful frame of mind, and that will benefit you as you move on to the next hole.

93.

Play a Round
Without a Scorecard

An interesting way to approach golf and play it for the love of the game is to eliminate one of the things that causes players the most irritation and frustration: keeping score. Yes, this is highly unusual, but if you try this, you might find that some elements disappear from the game—like stress, frustration, and irritation.

An earlier strategy in this book discussed the idea that while improving your score is one of your goals in golf, obsessing about the numbers can take away the real fun of the game. The easiest way to prove this theory is to simply play a round without keeping score. At first, you'll probably find yourself keeping score in your head. After all, being concerned with the numbers is a habit. But if you keep at it and try to concentrate on the other aspects of the game that really bring you pleasure, you may find that you lose your place and decide to quit counting after all.

Try putting your mind on the beauty and challenge of the course you're playing. Does the seventh hole suddenly seem less daunting? Does the bunker 200 yards off the tee seem placed there to punish, or is it there to pose an interesting obstacle to maneuver around? Enjoy the environment all around you. Many courses are carved out of the beauty of nature. You might find that you're playing pretty well when you're doing it for the sheer pleasure rather than the score.

You may think playing without keeping score is a crazy idea, but it's worth giving it a shot—or many shots, if you can keep yourself from adding them up. You may find that a bad start to your game is less likely to ruin your whole round, and you may even welcome unusual situations when you don't have to be concerned with the numbers.

94.

Play a Round
Without a Full Set of Irons

At first, the idea of playing without a full set of irons may seem odd, but if visualizing shots is frustrating to you and you're struggling with the creative aspect of golf, this strategy can help you relax and let your natural talents and abilities take over. Players can lock themselves into notions about which club to use for which situation, and recite them as rules: "Use the 5-iron from 160 yards, use the 8-iron from 130...." This mechanical mindset can make it difficult to visualize shots with in-between distances or strokes that require an unusual flight pattern. A 138-yard shot isn't quite an 8-iron, but it's not a 7-iron, either. If you're stuck on the "rules," you'll have problems inventing this shot or creating one to help you recover from the trees.

For mental flexibility, try playing one round with only your odd-numbered irons. You'll be forced to be creative with what you've got. For shots where you'd normally hit an 8-iron, try a 7-iron.

Swing it easier and hit a softer shot—this helps create tempo, develops feel and touch, and improves your creativity. Later, play another round with only your even-numbered irons. Then try only woods, or low-number irons—there are many ways to vary your practice. Some teachers advocate going out with only one club! It doesn't matter which one, just putt with it, chip with it, drive with it—do it all, even if the one club is your 5-iron.

Some players won't try this because they don't want others to see them doing something strange, or because they have to turn in a score. If either excuse is one that you've used, it could be a sign that you've lost your ability to play for pure fun. Remember that the creative side of golf is what makes it so interesting, and it's something that the great players relish. They love the challenge of trying to create a new shot that they've never thought of, or coming up with a way to deal with a situation that others would consider a bad break.

So try something different by practicing with only a few clubs. Golf isn't a science—it's an art. Being creative in your practice means that you'll become more creative when faced with those in-between shots and other unexpected things that the game can throw at you.

95.

Save the Analysis
for After the Round

Analyzing your game while you're still playing can have disastrous effects. You'll probably start beating yourself up before too long. Negative thoughts usually dominate, such as, "I'm so bad that I can't do this right. Why can't I ever play this course?"

Face it: Your analysis rarely takes into account the things that you're doing well. When you're focusing on the negative things, you can make yourself or your partners tense and irritable. This is why it's best to put off any analyzing until after the round, when the game is over and done with, and you don't risk making any problems worse.

It takes practice to get out of the habit of analyzing during a round. If you find analysis creeping into your thoughts while you're still playing, gently set those thoughts aside. Refocus yourself on the shot at hand, and don't be in such a hurry to pick apart every move that you've made. There's plenty of time for that, but you have only eighteen holes to enjoy and have fun.

96.

Avoid Practicing
After a Bad Round

You know those days when nothing that you do on the golf course feels right. The club feels lousy, your muscles feel tight, maybe your shoes are uncomfortable—and every hole looks impossible. It's amazing how many golfers will then head to the practice range to try to make adjustments after having such a bad day. If you want to save yourself pain and frustration, put the clubs away and try again tomorrow. There's no reason to continue to upset yourself.

You don't have to feel guilty for skipping practice after a bad round. Just remind yourself that trying to practice after a day of snap-hooked tee shots or hitting all of your iron shots off the hozzle may tend to make things worse. It's always tempting to go "work it out" on the practice range right away, but it's really best to let it go and save making adjustments for a new day. A bad round can leave you looking at yourself and your game through the wrong-colored glasses, and waiting until the next day can clear up your perspective.

It's easier to correct problems when you've got a good handle on them and where they're coming from. Time can help you understand those things.

The key is to tune into your body and listen to what it's telling you. Were you having a bad day because your body didn't feel right? If that's the case, practice can make you feel worse. Only when you can feel positive and informed in your analysis of your bad round, can you work some things out in practice.

97.

Get Over the
First-Tee Jitters

Every golfer has felt the "first-tee jitters." Preparing for your first shot of the day can be quite nerve-racking. The first tee is often where you set the tone for your round. If you give in to the jitters, the day could turn out to be just the opposite of the relaxing, enjoyable game of golf that you had in mind.

Sure, there are usually more people watching you on the first tee than anywhere else on the course, and that can cause many golfers to feel anxious. Even worse, the first tee may be in sight of the clubhouse, making you feel as if you're teeing off in a goldfish bowl, surrounded by others that you think are prepared to critique every nuance of your form and movement. Playing with people with whom you haven't played before might also make you jittery. There are plenty of possibilities for tension, but there are also some good ways to relieve those jitters.

One trick for getting over the first-tee jitters is to remember that many of the other golfers are probably feeling the same way! In fact, they're probably so focused on their own concerns that they're not paying much attention to you as you tee up. But even if you are the center of attention for some of the crowd, keep in mind that all it takes is for fifteen minutes to pass, and nobody will remember where you hit your ball or how you hit it. Even if you slice it, top it, or break a window in somebody's kitchen, the other players will have problems of their own to focus on soon enough, and they'll forget about you.

The best way to overcome the jitters, however, is to not allow yourself to care about what others think in the first place. Deciding to play your game your way and for your own enjoyment can eliminate any need that you may have for the approval of others. Keep in mind that it simply doesn't matter what other players might be thinking as you tee up. When you realize this, you'll feel less self-conscious and more eager to simply get to your game. If you tend to get the first-tee jitters, you probably won't eliminate the problem overnight. Practice concentrating on what's important—your shot, not those watching it.

98.

Let Your Kids Play

Getting your kids interested in golf and letting them play is a terrific way to develop an activity that you can enjoy together as a family. Watching tournaments, going to the practice range, and even playing a round together now and then can bring you and your children closer by giving you something in common.

Kids need to learn certain fundamentals from the start, but it's not necessary to bog them down with lessons. In fact, you can show them the basics of stance, grip, and swing, teach them fundamental rules, and let them go. Those who learn the game at a very young age often have the ability to mimic others quite well. If they watch good players swing and can absorb what they see, the good mimics are more likely to develop better swings in this manner than if they took lessons.

If your seven-year-old daughter is slamming them down the middle of the fairway, that's great! Let her play, and don't try to make her perfect. Don't take advice from others about her skills. If she's hitting them well, leave her alone! Let her talent develop naturally. Give kids a set of clubs and turn them loose—and let them watch other people play. Caddying for good players and watching tournaments are good ways for them to absorb habits on tempo, swing, and even etiquette.

The argument between those who believe that you must take lessons and those who believe that you can be self-taught has long been a part of modern golf debate, and eloquent points can be made for both sides. The truth is that genuine naturals are hard to find. Golf lessons are an important stepping stone for beginners and midlevel players looking to get to the next level. But it's not necessary to rush kids, either. Letting them experiment on their own can allow them to develop a creative approach to golf and make the game something that they want to play, rather than something that they do because they think you want them to do it. The kids will continue to play the game and learn, and that will make everyone happier.

99.

Remember the
Spirit of the Game

What makes golf the greatest game of all? It's a combination of qualities that keep new players learning the game and old players coming back to the course. Camaraderie makes it fun and competition makes it challenging, but the real spirit of the game is all about having fun.

That's always been the spirit of the game. Unfortunately, golfers can lose sight of it. They can become obsessed with numbers, such as hole lengths, par, handicaps, course ratings, and scoring. Players want to practice and improve their games, but many can become practice junkies, spending far too much time on the practice range and almost no time at all simply playing the game. There's a feeling that improvement is paramount because the game can be so punishing. You may have heard yourself say, "I play golf to shoot the best possible score that I can." If that's your real reason for playing, it's an unfortunate approach. Always remember that there's more to golf than scoring.

The distinguished Dr. Alister MacKenzie wrote in his posthumously published masterpiece, *The Spirit of St. Andrews:* "I believe that one gets far more fun in playing a match for five or ten dollars and licking one's opponent by lofting a stymie on the last green than you can ever get in taking your score. In Scotland, on completing a round, no one ever asked you, 'What is your score?' It is always, 'Did you beat him?' or 'Was it a tight match?'" Food for thought, to be sure.

You may hope to improve and lower your score, but at the same time, you don't want to get so caught up that you lose sight of the enjoyment of the game. That means breathing in the fresh air, taking in nature, and getting some healthy exercise. It also means not feeling like you have to play a complete round, but getting out there for the fun of hitting one or two shots and having a good time playing with your friends. It may sound like a simplification of the game and why you play it, but maybe it's what everyone needs to get back to, in this day and age of $500 titanium drivers, $52 boxes of a dozen balls, and swing gadgets galore.

Never lose sight of the fun of playing golf. It truly is why you took up the game in the first place. As long as you can have fun playing, you'll keep the true spirit of the game alive.

100.

Again, Remember
That It's Just a Game

You probably know a few golfers whose clubs are gathering dust in closets at home. You used to see them on the course—perhaps you played a regular round with them—but for some reason, they stopped playing. Players come and players go—they take up the game and leave it, often without really knowing why. Could it be that the fun has been wrung out of it for them—that they've forgotten that it's just a game? If you think back, you may see how their exodus from golf began, and indeed, you may discover that letting small things bother them had a lot to do with it.

Nobody starts playing golf to become irritated, frustrated, upset, anxious, uptight, injured, or exasperated. Initially, people take up the game to have fun, play with old friends, make new ones, get some exercise, and enjoy themselves. Somewhere along the line, many golfers become too serious about their games, and that's where the fun gets lost. If this sounds like what happened to those people that you don't see at your home course anymore, then take note.

It's been said that life is too important to take too seriously—if that's true, then certainly there's little or no reason to take golf too seriously. You can waste a lot of time and energy feeling stressed out and tense, when you could laugh it all off and have more fun. It all comes down to a choice, and the choice is always yours. If you really love the game of golf, you can make a conscious decision now to play for the reasons that you first started, and make every effort to enjoy playing to the fullest before you get carried away.

Tom Watson has said, "Golf will grow as long as it's fun." Those are poignant words to the wise. Golf is a great game that has enjoyed a resurgence and revitalization. If it's affordable for most people, it's fun to watch on television and in person, and there are enough interesting courses that make you want to come back, that will probably be enough to sustain the sport. There's one vital element that will ensure that golf will always remain "cool," and that's the element of fun. As long as you, the players, make sure that you always find your fun in the game, there will always be a game to play.